THE BEST OF THE

NBA

Jack Clary

THE BEST OF THE NBA

Jack Clary

BISON GROUP

First published in 1994 by
Bison Books Ltd.
Kimbolton House
117A Fulham Road
London SW3 6RL

ISBN 1-85841-132-7

Printed in China

Page 1: Power forward Larry Johnson of the Charlotte Hornets.

Page 2 (clockwise from top left): George Mikan (in glasses) and the 1949
Minneapolis Lakers; Shaq Attack – Shaquille O'Neal; one of the NBA's
ultimate rivalries: the Celtics' Larry Bird and the Lakers' Magic Johnson,
1987; the legendary Wilt Chamberlain.

Page 3 (clockwise from top left): "Dr. J" – Julius Erving; the Charlotte
Hornets' Alonzo Mourning; Patrick Ewing drives past Bulls center Bill
Cartwright; Magic Johnson (left) and Michael Jordan on the 1992 U.S.
Olympic Dream Team.

These pages: NBA jam: the Seattle Supersonics' Shawn Kemp does the
business against the Denver Nuggets.

Contents

INTRODUCTION

In the dynamic hierarchy of NBA basketball, the only constant is change. Michael Jordan is gone, but David Robinson is poised to take his place. So are Scottie Pippen, Hakeem Olajuwon, Danny Manning, Cliff Robinson, Patrick Ewing, Dominique Wilkins and Karl Malone.

Impatient youth in the presence of Shaquille O'Neal has arrived. So have Alonzo Mourning, Chris Webber, Anfernee Hardaway, Shawn Kemp, Glen Rice, Latrell Sprewell and Gary Payton.

The Chicago Bulls dynasty lasted three years, and the Orlando Magic and Seattle Supersonics are poised to make a run for the top. But first they must overcome the New York Knicks, Houston Rockets and Utah Jazz.

Pushing them are the Indiana Pacers, Charlotte Hornets, Miami Heat, and Golden State Warriors – and maybe even the New Jersey Nets and Denver Nuggets.

That's the beauty of the NBA. There is a constant ebb and flow of great players and great teams vying for recognition. When Jordan suddenly announced his retirement before the 1994 season, he was deemed indispensable, and the game was supposed to have suffered an irreplaceable loss.

There is no doubt that pro basketball lost its greatest player; that the athleticism and competitive intensity he brought to the games were missed. It has always been that way when the game's legends – from Bill Russell and Jerry West to Kareem Abdul-Jabbar, Magic Johnson and Larry Bird – have stepped away. But neither their loss, nor Jordan's, dimmed the luster of the game because the race to the top just intensified.

New young stars like O'Neal and Mourning promise to bring renewed emphasis to the "big man" in pro basketball. There is every indication that the fabulous Russell-Chamberlain battles of the 60s again will be reenacted when O'Neal

Above: Shawn Bradley of the Philadelphia 76ers tried to take the ball from the Houston Rockets' Hakeem Olajuwon in November 1993. ·

Left: Lakers legend Wilt Chamberlain (13) watches the ball part the twine as the Celtics take Game 4 of the 1969 NBA Finals.

Opposite left: Dr. J displays his famous sky hook against the Boston Celtics in 1985.

Opposite right: Michael Jordan takes to the air for one of his patented slam dunks in 1992 post-season action.

and Mourning face each other; or when they play against Robinson and Olajuwon and Ewing.

And a couple of generations hence, people will look back and celebrate those rivalries and showcase performances just as we still remember Russell-Chamberlain, the Celtics-Lakers of the 60s and 80s, the amazing flights of Julius Erving – and yes, those of Michael Jordan. The NBA will continue to captivate us with amazing games and individual feats. When the NBA tallies its eight millionth point shortly after the millenium the grainy black-and-white films of its early seasons will still be as interesting as the feats of its pioneers.

The game continues to grow. New Orleans may again welcome an NBA team, and Toronto will host an NBA team for the first time in nearly a half century. The international flow of players has brought rookies Tony Kukoc to Chicago and Dino Radja to the Celtics, as they join other European stars who have carved their niches.

Within a year, such new players as Glenn Robinson, Grant Hill, Jason Kidd, Donyell Marshall, Jalen Rose, Melvin Booker, Khalid Reeves and Cliff Rozier will begin to push such recent stars as Orlando's Hardaway, Webber of Golden State, Isaiah Rider of Minnesota, the 76ers' Shawn Bradley, Jamaal Mashburn of the Dallas Mavericks, Vin Baker of Milwaukee, Nick Van Exel of the Lakers and Lindsey Hunter of Detroit, all of whom barely have gotten their NBA feet wet.

Already the NBA is preparing to defend its 1992 Dream Team Olympic Gold Medal in the 1996 Olympic Games in Atlanta with the formation of Dream Team II – a team that competed in the summer of 1994 in Toronto at the International Basketball Championships.

In the rivalries between teams and players and the continual changing of the guard that distinguish NBA competition, skilled and colorful athletes continue to make their marks in the history of the game.

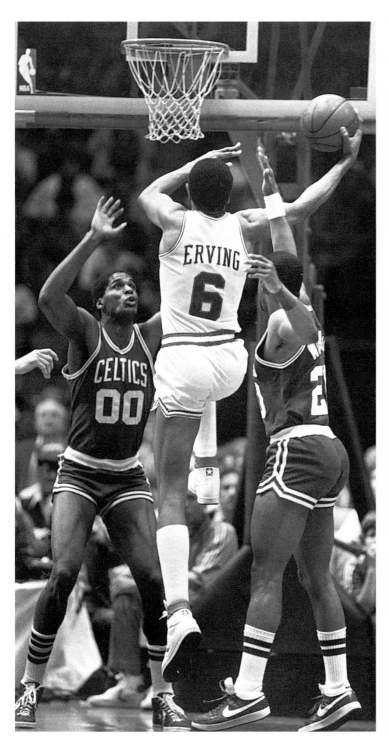

THE NBA's BEST AND BRIGHTEST

When non-centers like Michael Jordan, Larry Bird, Kevin McHale, Karl Malone, Charles Barkley, Isiah Thomas and Magic Johnson ruled the NBA during the 80s and early 90s, the big men – the centers – took a back seat.

No longer.

The dominant players are now the Houston Rockets' Hakeem Olajuwon, the NBA's 1994 Most Valuable Player; the game's two brightest newcomers, Shaquille O'Neal of Orlando and Alonzo Mourning of Charlotte; David Robinson of San Antonio; and Patrick Ewing of the Knicks, who like Olajuwon, bridges the former era.

There still are "franchise" non-centers, including forwards Malone and Barkley, as well as Chicago's Scottie Pippen, Dominique Wilkins of the Clippers and Shawn Kemp of Seattle; and some guards in the same strata, like John Stockton of Utah, Mark Price of Cleveland, Kevin Johnson of Phoenix, Mitch Richmond of Sacramento, Reggie Miller of Indiana and Latrell Sprewell of Golden State. But none of them is in a class with the dominant centers to whom this chapter is devoted.

O'Neal and Mourning came into the NBA together and it appears they will challenge each other for supremacy for the rest of their careers. At 6'10", 240 pounds, Alonzo is not as big as O'Neal, but there has been just the barest shade of difference between their abilities. O'Neal edged Mourning as 1993 Rookie of the Year but both were unanimous picks for the NBA's All-Rookie team.

Robinson had begun to dip until the 1994 season when he brought his game up a couple of notches, won the NBA's scoring title and formed the league's best rebound-ing duo with Dennis Rodman (they combined for 28 per game). Many believe he is capable of being the game's best all-around center if he continues to stretch his abilities.

Olajuwon and Ewing have been dueling each other ever since the 1984 NCAA championship game. They met at the 1994 NBA Finals, when Hakeem led Houston to its first championship and was named MVP of the playoffs. Still possessing outstanding athletic ability, but seasoned with savvy, the two veterans continue to bring the game – and their teams – to new heights.

Below left: Two of the NBA's best, Patrick Ewing of the New York Knicks and Hakeem Olajuwon of the Houston Rockets, go head to head in the 1994 NBA Finals.

Below: The 1994 scoring champion, David Robinson.

PATRICK EWING

Until 1985, the NBA always allowed the team with the worst record to select first in the annual draft of college players.

But Patrick Ewing, a seven-foot, 240-pound center, who was a three-time All-America at Georgetown and led the Hoyas to the 1984 NCAA Championship (as well as two other visits to the NCAA Finals), was so coveted that the league established its lottery system for selecting the top picks to prevent any team during the 1985 season from deliberately creating the worst record to secure his services.

Now that shows respect, and while some, particularly fans of the New York Knicks who won the first lottery, may carp because he didn't deliver immediate championships,

he has established himself as one of the NBA's great players and today owns every important offensive record in the team's nearly half century.

Most of all, he has worked as hard as anyone in the game's history to achieve his stardom. He has been in the public eye since his high school years in Cambridge, Massachusetts, and while he was a fine player during those years, he was far from a great one.

"People said he had a lot of natural talent but he was not a natural talent at basketball," said one observer who has known him since his freshman year at Georgetown. "He's gotten better every year. He came into the NBA as a defensive player, and he worked hard to elevate his game to a new dimension. Now he averages 25 points a game, pulls

Left: Ewing vs. Hakeem Olajuwon in the 1994 NBA Finals. Despite Ewing's fine performance the Knicks were beaten in seven games by the Houston Rockets.

Above: Ewing battles Kareem Abdul-Jabbar of the Los Angeles Lakers in 1985. Like Jabbar when he entered the NBA back in the late '60s, Ewing was projected to become a superstar center capable of making his team a continual title contender, and of ultimately succeeding Kareem as the league's top player.

Left: New York Knicks fans expected so much of Patrick Ewing that when he didn't deliver a string of instant championships, he did not enjoy the same love and affection once accorded Walt Frazier (right), who led New York to its first world championship back in 1970.

Below: One of Ewing's biggest nemeses was the Chicago Bulls, led by Michael Jordan. Until 1994, the Bulls had thrice deprived the Knicks of a championship game slot.

Opposite: Ewing does battle with the NBA's new "big kid on the block," Shaquille O'Neal of the Orlando Magic, who came into the league with the same tag of championship potential Ewing had arrived with back in 1985.

down rebounds by the dozens and still has his great defensive skills."

Ewing is one of those players who is victimized by his "potential." He was a dominating player at the high school and college levels but he had to work on his scoring to fulfill the expectations laid on him as a "franchise player."

Because his is a very private person and does not suffer the media with any relish, few have ever gotten keen insights into what makes him function.

"You have to realize," noted Boston Celtics President Red Auerbach, who tutored the game's greatest all-around center, Bill Russell, "that the hardest thing in basketball is to be the best player on a team that's not very good. And yet what I like about him is that he gives a champion's effort every time out. Every time."

In 1994, Ewing hit two important milestones – he became the 68th player in NBA history to score 15,000 points, and three months later, he became the 55th player to score 16,000 points. He also became the Knicks' all-time leading scorer, surpassing Walt Frazier's record, and rang up arguably his finest season with epic performances. He had 15 consecutive 20-point games, missed one, and then rang up 17 more in a row. He also had 19 games where he scored 30 or more points, and two games with more than 40 points. When he hits 30 or more, the Knicks are 14-5 during his career; when he scores more than 40, they are 27-0.

And that doesn't even account for the rebounds that same season: 18 games with more than 20 en route to the club leadership.

Now that's an impact player.

ALONZO MOURNING

Alonzo Mourning, after just two NBA seasons, had made his mark as center for the Charlotte Hornets. He not only was selected to the NBA All-Star team in 1994 for the first time, but the savvy basketball trendies and the cable TV sports shows now refer to him as "Zo," a shortened form of his first name. That conveys a fond familiarity in this new age of verbal abbreviations.

Mourning proved his worth during the 1994 season when he was forced to carry the team's offensive load after Larry Johnson was slowed with injuries. His value was proven with two statistics: when Mourning played, the Hornets were 35-25; in the 22 games he missed, the club was 6-16.

Mourning surprised many with his accelerated offensive game, because centers from Georgetown (Patrick Ewing and Dikembe Mutombo) do not come into the NBA with reputations as great scorers. Mourning was no slouch because he finished 1994 as only the second player in Georgetown history (along with Patrick Ewing) to collect more than 2,000 points (2,001) and 1,000 rebounds (1,032) in a season; and he ranked second behind Mutombo in blocked shots.

Mourning began his NBA career with a fine 1993 rookie season, finishing as runner-up for NBA Rookie of the Year. He averaged more than 20 points per game and 10

Above: Alonzo Mourning (33) of the Charlotte Hornets, seen here battling Rik Smits of Indiana, is another in a line of great centers from Georgetown, including Patrick Ewing of the New York Knicks and Dikembe Mutombo of the Denver Nuggets.

Left: Mourning wears the same jersey number – 33 – as his boyhood idol Ewing, who also tutored him when he played at Georgetown. He became an instant force in the middle for the Hornets and brought them to the playoffs during his rookie season in 1993.

Opposite: To pro basketball's "in" crowd, he's known as "Zo."

rebounds; and his 271 blocked shots were more than the total of the first two Charlotte teams combined.

He improved all of those numbers in 1994, but without having Larry Johnson as an impact player to help relieve the pressure from opposing defenses, as was the case in 1993. "Zo" led his team in scoring with a 21.5 points per game average; in rebounding with 10.1; and in blocked shots with 3.13, fourth best in the NBA. In 39 of his 60 games, he scored 20 or more points, and he had more than 30 points in six of those.

But what has impressed everyone in the NBA is his willingness to work. The 6'10", 240-pounder from Chesapeake, Virginia, willingly mixes it up with every big man in the league. In 1994 he had 38 games with 10 or more rebounds, and in five of those, he had more than 15 rebounds.

He also was fourth among the Hornets in foul attempts, which meant that he was forcing teams to counter his work in the pivot.

Mourning was picked for Dream Team II, which represented the United States in the World Championship Games during the summer of 1994 as a prelude to the 1996 Olympic Games in Atlanta.

HAKEEM OLAJUWON

Hakeem Olajuwon, nicknamed "Hakeem the Dream," has become the "Nigerian Nightmare" for anyone contesting "the paint" – that area around the basket that centers carve out as their exclusive domain.

For the second consecutive season Olajuwon, a native of Lagos, Nigeria, was selected by the NBA's coaches as the league's top defensive center in 1994, and he was also picked as the best defensive player in voting by media from around the league.

Olajuwon has always been a fine defensive player, and while seeming to get better at that most difficult of all skills, he has become an all-out offensive force. He had the best season of his career in 1994 with a 27.3 average on 2,184 points, third in the NBA. He also was among the top 10 players in field goal percentage, and received the ultimate recognition when he was chosen as the league's Most Valuable Player, and MVP in the playoffs.

"He now dominates both ends of the floor," said one NBA coach, "and that is a fearsome prospect. At one time, you didn't underline his offense, but he now brings the entire package to the game."

Chris Ford, the Celtics coach, has noted, "Hakeem is big enough to battle other centers head-up; and on offense, he can overpower a big man who cannot match his quickness and leaping ability."

That same quickness and leaping ability mark his defen-

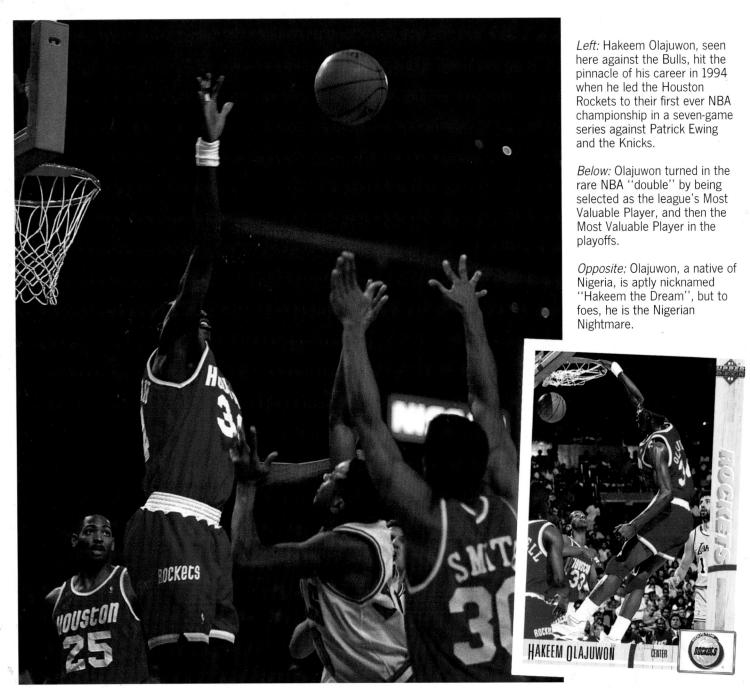

Left: Hakeem Olajuwon, seen here against the Bulls, hit the pinnacle of his career in 1994 when he led the Houston Rockets to their first ever NBA championship in a seven-game series against Patrick Ewing and the Knicks.

Below: Olajuwon turned in the rare NBA "double" by being selected as the league's Most Valuable Player, and then the Most Valuable Player in the playoffs.

Opposite: Olajuwon, a native of Nigeria, is aptly nicknamed "Hakeem the Dream", but to foes, he is the Nigerian Nightmare.

HAKEEM OLAJUWON   CENTER

Opposite: Hakeem Olajuwon starred as a collegian for the University of Houston famed Phi Slama Jama run-and-gun team of the early 80s. He led them to the NCAA Finals but lost to Georgetown and Patrick Ewing in his junior year, though he was picked as the tournament's MVP in part because of the same kind of defense he displays here against the Knicks' Mark Jackson.

Right: Olajuwon became only the fourth player in NBA history ever named the league's Defensive Player of the Year in back-to-back seasons when he won the award in 1993-94. He holds the team record for most blocked shots, and proved his versatility by also recording more steals than any player in the team's history.

sive skills. He is an awesome physical specimen at seven feet, 255 pounds; he is one of the most athletic centers in the NBA as displayed by his remarkable shot-blocking totals. Olajuwon is the first player ever to block 200 or more shots a year for 10 straight years (since the NBA began keeping blocks as an official statistic in 1974), and he now ranks third behind Kareem Abdul-Jabbar and Mark Eaton among NBA career leaders with 2,471.

Olajuwon was the big reason why the Rockets set a new franchise record for the fewest points allowed and in field goal defense during the 1994 season. He was fourth in the NBA in rebounds with nearly 12 a game (726 total) in the 1994 season.

Racking up career milestones, in the 1994 season Hakeem became the third player in NBA history to record 10,000 points, 5,000 rebounds and 1,000 steals, assists and blocked shots.

Olajuwon has been steadily living up to the potential that was obvious when he was the first player picked in the 1984 NBA draft after a great All-American season at the University of Houston. A member of Houston's famed "Phi Slama Jama" NCAA Final Four team in 1983, he was later selected as the Southwest Conference's Player of the Eighties.

SHAQUILLE O'NEAL

The NBA is under constant siege from a Shaq attack.

Shaquille O'Neal has become pro basketball's newest impact player – on and off the court – and he has stepped in as its cover boy following the retirement of Michael Jordan.

O'Neal is a force. He is 7'1" and 303 pounds, and he throws that size around with reckless abandon. Battling more experienced centers to a standstill, if not overwhelming them on occasion, he totally dominates everyone else. Some NBA observers call him the most physically dominant center since Wilt Chamberlain came into the NBA in 1960.

The force of O'Neal's play also has made some wonder just how good he can get given the fact that he has played to All-Star dimensions in his first two seasons.

Often young players who have dynamic rookie years will slump in their second year as opposing defenses get a line on them and they relax the intensity of trying to prove themselves. That was not the case during O'Neal's second year in 1994. He led the NBA in field goal accuracy with 59.9 percent; he was second in scoring with a 29.3 points per game average, on 2,377 points (he scored 1,893 for a

Above: Shaquille O'Neal was an All-America center at Louisiana State University before becoming the first pick for the 1993 NBA season by the Orlando Magic.

Left: O'Neal has quickly become one of the NBA's most powerful offensive forces. In 1994, just his second season, he scored 40 or more points eight times and finished second in scoring with a 29.3 average, and also was second in rebounds.

Opposite: Midway through his rookie season in 1993, O'Neal was named starting center for the Eastern Conference in the NBA's All-Star game in 1994. Here he is seen duelling with Karl Malone.

23.3 mark as a rookie); he scored 40 or more points eight times and his sophomore average was just a half point behind NBA leader David Robinson; he was second in rebounds with a 13.2 average on 1,072; and he was sixth in blocked shots with nearly three a game.

What did this mean on a per game basis? He led the Orlando Magic in scoring 55 times, he led his team in rebounds 73 times, and there were only five games in which he didn't block a shot. He also led the NBA with 65 double-doubles (doubles figure in scoring and rebounding).

He scored a personal and franchise record 53 points against Minnesota in just 36 minutes of play. He tried to put to flight any questions about his endurance in light of his 300 pounds, going 53 minutes in Boston five days before his record-setting performance against the Timberwolves.

Off the court, O'Neal has been an even bigger hit. He is now the most sought after professional athlete in the endorsement game, and he even has one advertisement projecting him as "Grandpa Shaq." But long before he ever reaches that exalted status, he may well completely redefine the center position in basketball.

Opposite: Alonzo Mourning (33) and Shaquille O'Neal are the two best young centers in the NBA and their battles have already become legendary in the same manner as those once waged by Bill Russell and Wilt Chamberlain during the 60s.

Above right: O'Neal led the Magic into the playoffs for the first time ever in 1994, and turned in prodigious figures — he led the team in scoring 55 times; in rebounds 73 times; and he led the NBA in double-doubles with 65.

Right: O'Neal is a walking conglomerate with more than $70 million in endorsements and salary, and he has become one of the nation's most visible personalities.

DAVID ROBINSON

David Robinson has established his own exclusive neighborhood in a land of NBA giants.

Robinson, the 7'1", 235-pound center for the San Antonio Spurs, plays with great talent and a grace that belies the way he dominates his area of the court. Robinson's fierce determination is often lost on those who are deceived by the great ease with which he appears to play the game.

A Naval Academy graduate, Robinson grew so much during his four years as a midshipman that he surpassed the height limit for naval service and was excused from active duty after just two years. "The Admiral" has been the biggest force in carrying the Spurs to the playoffs during each of his first four years, beginning in 1990.

In 1994 he won his first NBA scoring title with a 29.8 average – the first center to win a crown in 18 years, since Bob McAdoo, and only the sixth center in NBA history to win scoring honors.

But it was the manner in which he did it – with a tremendous, 71-point performance in the season's final game against the Los Angeles Clippers – that showed the stuff of which he is made. It was only the fourth time in NBA history that a player has surpassed 70 points, but Robinson was so determined not to lose the title to Shaquille O'Neal that he literally destroyed the Clippers by himself.

This overt bit of fire is something new for Robinson, but it is also emblematic of how he has elevated his game to greater heights because he has been challenged by new

Left: David Robinson was the greatest player in Navy's basketball history. He grew seven inches during his four years at the Naval Academy, going from a small forward to the most dominating center in college basketball in 1987.

Above: Robinson receives the Wooden Award from its namesake, former UCLA coach John Wooden, as the top college player of the 1987 season.

Opposite: "Mr. Robinson's Neighborhood" around the San Antonio Spurs' basket welcomes no visitors, not even a superstar like Dominique Wilkins.

young centers like O'Neal, Denver's Dikembe Mutombo and Alonzo Mourning of Charlotte.

In 1994 Robinson became only the third player in league history to rank among the top 30 in six major statistical categories (first in scoring, third in blocked shots; 14th in rebounds; 19th in steals; 20th in field goal percentage; and 29th in assists). Further, he was the league's top foul shooter.

"David's got so much talent it's ridiculous," said teammate Dennis Rodman.

That talent is pivotal to his team. For example, Robinson scored 40 or more points seven times during the 1994 season and San Antonio won every game; and he scored more than 30 points 41 times during that season and the Spurs, who are not a talent-laden team, won 30 of those games. He has scored in double figures in 388 of his 394 games thus far.

While still acknowledged as one of the "gentlemen" of the NBA, Robinson has always been a great defensive force. He was the NBA's Defensive Player of the Year in 1992, when he also led the league in blocked shots. He narrowly missed winning that accolade again in 1994 by just one vote.

Top: David Robinson was a member of the 1992 U.S. Olympic gold medal team.

Left: Robinson won his first NBA scoring title in 1994 with an incredible 71-point effort in the season's final game.

Above: "The Admiral".

Opposite: Robinson was named Rookie of the Year in 1990.

STARS OF THE NBA

The best players in the NBA are the best basketball players in the world.

They are the players who can shoot with great accuracy; pass with great skill; defend with great intensity; and approach every game with the mindset that they will be the very best they can be.

The Hall of Fame is filled with them. They are the ones who appear each year in the NBA's All-Star Game and on the year-end All-NBA team. Most importantly, they are the ones who have helped their teams into the playoffs.

The league's great centers are featured in the previous chapter, but right with them is a group that includes such long-time stars as Karl Malone, Charles Barkley, Joe Dumars, Scottie Pippen, Dominique Wilkins, Kevin Johnson and John Stockton. Four of this star-studded group –

Malone, Barkley, Pippin and Stockton – were recognized for their skills as members of the 1992 Dream Team in the Olympic Games.

But in the continual parade of NBA talent, new players have begun to make their mark. There is Gary Payton of Seattle, a member of the league's all-defensive team and a double-digit scorer. Then there is Glen Rice of Miami, who helped to turn around his teams and get them into the playoffs, Indiana's Rik Smits, and great playmakers and scorers like Reggie Miller of Indiana, Danny Manning of Atlanta, Chicago's Horace Grant, Philadelphia's Jeff Hornacek, Cleveland's Mark Price and Sacramento's Mitch Richmond. Part of America's next generation of Olympians is represented by NBA stars Shawn Kemp, Price and Miller.

Left: Kevin Johnson (7).

Below: Horace Grant.

CHARLES BARKLEY

When Charles Barkley is healthy and on the move, he is one of the NBA's premier "body movers." Opponents scatter when he comes roaring down the lane to dunk a ball, or when he grabs a rebound and makes space on the way up for a shot.

At 6'6" and 252 pounds, he looks more like an NFL lineman than an NBA player, but his appearance masks some marvelous physical skills. Sometimes he becomes so overpowering that teammates depend on him too much. That may have been a factor during the 1994 playoffs when the Suns were eliminated in seven games by the Houston Rockets, and Barkley often found himself a one-man gang with little help.

During the 1992 Olympic Games in Barcelona, he put on a spectacular show for the United States "Dream Team"; and then during the 1993 season, he led the Phoenix Suns into the NBA Finals and won the league's Most Valuable Player Award.

Throughout his NBA career, which began in Philadelphia in 1985, he has averaged Hall of Fame numbers – 23.3 points per game and 870 rebounds a season. He has been named to the All-Star team eight times.

Barkley's fame has reached such heights that he now is one of the most popular professional athletes in the product endorsement business – always with an offbeat twist that suits his sometimes outrageous personality.

Right: Charles Barkley is a one-man band, a troubadour on and off the court who is apt to do anything in the midst of a game to attract attention. A gifted player especially for someone of such girth (6' 6", 252 pounds), he played for the Philadelphia 76ers for eight seasons and was an almost perennial All-Star selection, starting with his rookie year when he led Philadelphia into the Eastern Conference playoff finals. He averaged 20 or more points in seven of those eight years and was part of a monster trade that sent Jeff Hornacek from Phoenix to the 76ers after the 1992 season.

Left: Charles Barkley made himself the most visible member of the 1992 U.S. Olympic gold medal basketball team, on and off the court. He was also named by the nation's basketball writers to their "all interview" first team – unanimously in 1992-93 – in five of its first six years.

Above: In 1993, his first season with the Phoenix Suns after being traded from the Philadelphia 76ers, Barkley was selected as the NBA's Most Valuable Player after leading the Phoenix Suns into the NBA Finals.

Right: Barkley has been named to eight All-Star teams. In 1994, he led all players in voting with plays such as this one against Stacy King of the Chicago Bulls.

JOE DUMARS

Joe Dumars is the last vestige of the Detroit Pistons' championship team of the late 80s and 1990 when they won back-to-back NBA championships. Then, as now, he was always regarded as their steadiest player.

Dumars, a 6'3", 195-pound guard, has been a perennial selection to the NBA's all-defensive team, but for the past several seasons he also has been Detroit's chief offensive weapon. He has led the team in scoring four consecutive seasons, and his 23.5 average in 1993 has been exceeded by only five players in Pistons' history.

Joe was always the consummate team player in the Pistons' glory years, never seeking the spotlight nor provoking controversies as did teammates Isiah Thomas, Bill Laimbeer and Rick Mahorn with their roughhouse play.

Dumars, a first-round draft pick from McNeese State in Louisiana in 1985, has appeared in five straight NBA All-Star Games. He is one of the NBA's best foul shooters with better than 80 percent accuracy for seven straight seasons, and his durability is unquestioned with three consecutive years playing 3,000 or more minutes.

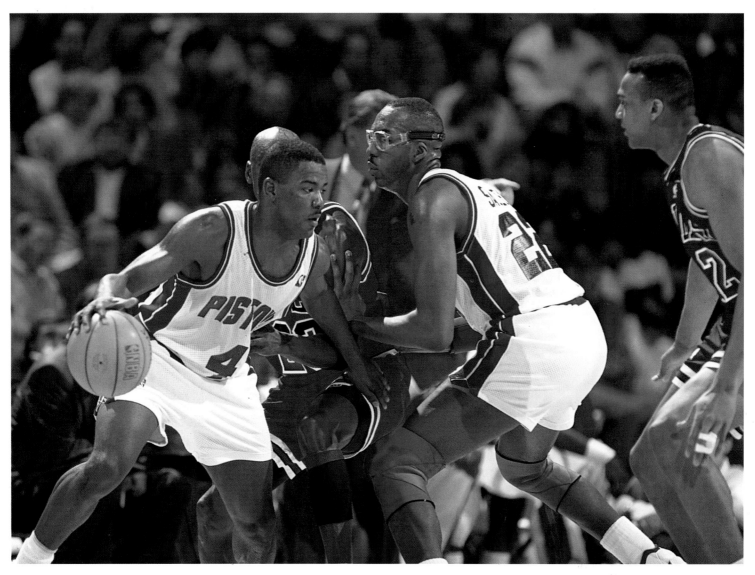

HORACE GRANT

Horace Grant takes a back seat to no one in casting an imposing shadow on the basketball court, despite having played with Michael Jordan and Scottie Pippen during his eight seasons with the Chicago Bulls.

Without Grant, the Bulls would not have won three straight NBA titles because he was their workhorse on the boards. In the Bulls' 1993 championship year, the 6'10", 235-pound forward who wears his trademark white goggles, led them in rebounding 39 times. He increased that to 43 in 1994. His ability to help control the offensive boards and put back missed shots has also contributed to his better-than-50 percent shooting mark in each of his NBA seasons.

And his ability as a shot blocker and rebounder also earned him a second consecutive spot on the NBA's all-defensive team in 1994.

With the departed Jordan's offensive load parceled out to more players in 1994, Grant, who began his NBA career as a number one draft pick from Clemson in 1987, stepped up and led the team in scoring 10 times, during which it was 8-2. He scored 20 points 11 times (compared to nine times in Jordan's final season) en route to 42 double-double games (double figures in scoring and rebounding); and he hit double figures in 62 of his 70 games.

Opposite top: Joe Dumars was an integral part of Detroit's two-time NBA champions in 1989-90, and was selected as MVP of the 1989 Finals against the Lakers.

Opposite below: Dumars was a perfect fit for Detroit's aggressive defensive style that smothered opponents. He was a three-time member of the NBA's all-defensive first team.

Right: Horace Grant was an unsung hero of the Chicago Bulls' three-time NBA champions because of his rebounding. He led the Bulls in rebounding for five consecutive seasons (1990-94), and he has never shot below 50 percent since joining the Bulls as a Number 1 pick in 1987.

JEFF HORNACEK

Jeff Hornacek is one of the NBA's best backcourt performers and it seems he always rises to the top when he is paired with similar great players – as in Phoenix when he and Kevin Johnson shared the backcourt, and as in 1994 in Utah when he moved in to work with guard John Stockton.

Hornacek, a 6'4", 190-pound guard from Iowa State who was a second-round draft pick of the Phoenix Suns in 1986, was just the man the Utah Jazz needed to boost them into the 1994 NBA playoffs because he bolstered a backcourt rotation that already included an All-Star in Stockton. Their playmaking put non-stop pressure on opposing defenses to try and cope with Utah's high-powered offense. It was one big reason why the team won eight of its final 10 games.

Hornacek, who was traded to Utah by Philadelphia in February 1994 after playing the season's first 53 games with the 76ers (he had come to the 76ers after the 1992 season in a blockbuster trade that sent Charles Barkley to the Phoenix Suns), wound up as the Jazz' number three scorer with a 14.6 average, and had a 15.9 mark for the entire season.

His 419 assists in 1994 were the fourth best of his career. During his career, he has led his teams in free throws, assists, steals and shooting percentage.

Left: Jeff Hornacek was traded from Philadelphia to the Utah Jazz during the 1994 season, and he added the needed touch to lead the team to the playoffs when he teamed with guard John Stockton.

Opposite top: Kevin Johnson turned down a major league baseball career to pursue basketball. He has become one of the NBA's premier playmakers, who also was picked as one of President George Bush's "1000 Points of Light" in 1989.

Opposite below: Johnson is a ferocious competitor. He turned in one of the NBA's greatest iron-man performances ever when he played 62 of the 63 minutes in a triple overtime playoff game for the Suns against the Chicago Bulls in 1993. Here he is seen wielding the ball between Jeff Malone and Mark Eaton of the Utah Jazz.

KEVIN JOHNSON

Kevin Johnson – KJ to millions of NBA fans – is one of the NBA's premier playmakers. Yet KJ giveth in the same measure that he taketh away. In 1994 he had the NBA's single game high of 25 assists and the league's single game high of 10 steals, one shy of tying the all-time record.

That deftness is typical of Johnson's great all-around talent that has made him an All-Star player in each of his first seven NBA seasons.

While many players rate their games by the number of times they hit double figures in scoring, Johnson measures his with the number of times he does it with assists *and* with his scoring. He had 10 or more assists 28 times during the 1994 season; and he hit the double figure scoring mark in all but two of the 67 games he played as he averaged 20 points per game. He had 30 or more points six times, and against the Denver Nuggets he scored 42 points – 29 in the first half – and doled out 17 assists.

He often is a "streak" player, as happened during the 1994 season when he hit double figures in scoring in 17 of his team's final 20 games.

Johnson, 6'1", 190 pounds, has accumulated 4,912 assists (nearly 10 per game) during his NBA career, which began in Cleveland in 1987, and he has 822 steals.

KJ's most memorable performance was playing 62 of the 63 minutes of a triple overtime playoff victory over the Chicago Bulls in the 1993 NBA Finals.

SHAWN KEMP

Just 19 years old when he was a first-round draft pick by Seattle in 1989, Kemp is one of only six players in NBA history ever to make it without the benefit of some major college experience.

The fact that he still is maturing and refining his game was shown by a much more aggressive style of play during the 1994 season. It has been a harder road for him, but he has reached the upper levels of competition and was a key force in helping his team to back-to-back playoffs in 1993-94.

Kemp, 6'10", 245 pounds, has blossomed into one of the league's best rebounders. He led the Supersonics in rebounding 60 times during the 1994 season, and ranked 13th in the NBA with 851, a 10.8 per game mark.

He also ranks third among all-time Seattle players in blocked shots. He led his team in rebounds and blocked shots in four of his first five seasons.

Kemp has developed some good offensive touches. He had 47 double-doubles during the 1994 season – double figures in scoring and rebounding – and led his team in scoring 27 times, averaging 18.1 points.

He has gained recognition for being the first Seattle player named to play in back-to-back All-Star games since Jack Sikma; and for being named to the NBA's Dream Team II All-Stars that played during the summer of 1994 in the World Basketball Championships in Toronto.

KARL MALONE

Karl Malone is one "Mailman" who has delivered in a big way for the Utah Jazz since his rookie 1986 season.

Nicknamed "The Mailman" because "he always delivers," Malone is one of the rare NBA players who has been a force unto himself since coming to Utah as a number one pick. Since then, he has averaged 20 points per game during eight of his first nine seasons, and in 1994 he scored his 19,000th career point.

Malone, 6′9″, 256 pounds, ranks as the all-time scorer and rebounder for the Jazz. In 1994 he scored more than 2,000 points for the seventh consecutive season. He also was a first team All-NBA selection as he led the team in scoring 69 times, and had 70 games of scoring 20 or more points. That season he led the Jazz in rebounds 57 times; and 50 times, he had more than 10 in a game.

Team president and former coach Frank Layden says Malone's biggest asset "is that he can catch the ball. He'll catch anything that's thrown to him, and then he lets his other skills take over."

That has been evident for years in the unique on-court dynamic that Malone has developed with guard John Stockton, the NBA's best playmaker. It barely takes a glance between the two to make a play.

Malone, who was a member of the U.S. Dream Team in the 1992 Olympic Games, also is very durable, having missed just four games during his first nine seasons.

Opposite: Shawn Kemp is one of just six NBA players who never had college experience. In 1994, he led the Seattle Supersonics in scoring 27 times, and in rebounding 60 times.

Above: Karl Malone has scored 2,000 points for seven straight seasons with the Utah Jazz. He also was a member of the U.S. Dream Team in the 1992 Olympic Games.

Right: Malone is one of the NBA's most rugged players, having played every game of the season six times during his first nine years in the league.

DANNY MANNING

Danny Manning was part of a trade involving NBA superstars when he was swapped by the Los Angeles Clippers to Atlanta for Dominique Wilkins midway through the 1994 season.

Despite his great talent, Manning has always shunned the limelight while still achieving his stardom. He knew he was expected to step up to the same level as Wilkins, one of the NBA's best players over the last decade.

He did so without fanfare, and certainly was a major factor in helping the Hawks win their division and tie for the best record in the Eastern Conference en route to the 1994 playoffs.

Manning, a 6′10″, 234-pound forward, has been labeled a potential franchise player since he was the NBA's number one pick in 1988 after helping Kansas win the NCAA championship. A serious knee injury set him back during his rookie season with the Clippers, but he has quietly worked his way toward the top echelon of NBA players.

In Atlanta he became more dominant. He led the team in scoring five times; in rebounding four times; in assists three times; and in steals six times.

"No one can say that Danny Manning does this or that better than anyone," said Larry Brown, his former coach at Kansas and with the Clippers. "But he does everything well and works hard, and he keeps getting better."

REGGIE MILLER

No one plays with more enthusiasm than Reggie Miller in games or in practices, or even shooting around on his driveway. He's a world class trash-talker on the court but he backs it up with his play as he helped the Pacers to the finals of the NBA's Eastern Conference playoffs in 1994 for the first time in their history.

Miller does it all as a guard. He scored the 10,000th point of his career in 1994 and he is the Indiana Pacers' all-time scorer. He led the team for the fifth year in a row with 1,574 points and a 19.9 average. He also had a club-high 13 game-winning points.

Reggie is one of the NBA's best three-point shooters, and when he is making them he seems to ignite the rest of his teammates, particularly center Rik Smits working around the basket. Miller is the fourth player in NBA history to hit more than 800 three-pointers.

Miller, 6'7", 185 pounds, and a number one pick in 1987 from UCLA, uses that same enthusiasm to direct the Pacers' offense. His 248 assists were third in the NBA in 1994. He also is an adept defender and he accumulated 119 steals in 1994, the fifth straight year in which he passed the 100 mark. He set a club record of 120 in 1993.

Reggie was chosen as a member of Dream II, the NBA All-Star team that played in the World Basketball Championship during the summer of 1994.

Opposite top: Danny Manning came to the Atlanta Hawks from the L.A. Clippers in the second half of the 1994 season and helped them to 18 wins in 25 games and a trip to the playoffs.

Opposite: The then-San Diego (later Los Angeles) Clippers made Manning (second from right) the first player selected in the 1988 draft after he led the Kansas Jayhawks to the NCAA championship. He was the Clippers' all-time scoring leader.

Top right: Reggie Miller is not only the Pacers' all-time leading scorer, but also one of the NBA's all-time leading trash-talkers, who takes on players and fans alike.

Right: Miller has the quickest hands in the NBA, having accumulated 100 steals for five straight years, and he also is one of the league's best foul shooters.

GARY PAYTON

Gary Payton was the first College Player of the Year the Seattle Supersonics ever drafted when they made him the second player selected in the first round of the 1990 NBA draft.

Payton, who also was the NCAA's all-time number two steal-maker during his career at Oregon State University, quickly made his mark as a premier playmaker when he got a personal single-game high of 16 assists during his rookie season.

He has since passed the 1,000-assist mark and fulfilled the promise of his rookie season when he led the Sonics, which had the NBA's best record in 1994, with 494 assists, a 6.0 average.

He didn't lose the knack for stealing the ball either, because he has accumulated more than 600 steals in four years.

In 1994 the 6'4", 190-pound Payton was selected to the NBA's all-pro team, and in the NBA All-Star Game he tabbed six points, six rebounds and nine assists.

His .504 shooting average (584 of 1,159) in 1994 was first among the league's point guards en route to his season total of 1,349 points for a 16.4 average, the best of his four-season career. The Sonics were 21-3 in 1994 when he scored 20 or more points.

Payton also is a very durable player; he missed just one game in his first four seasons.

Left: Gary Payton (center) has been an under-appreciated player everywhere in the NBA except in Seattle, where he has become the team's on-the-court leader with his playmaking and durability.

Opposite left: Scottie Pippen is a perennial member of the NBA's All-Defensive team. But his versatility also has caused many to term him a "point forward," because he brings a guard's style of play to the front court.

Opposite right: Pippen assumed Michael Jordan's role as the go-to guy for the Chicago Bulls, and in 1994 he led his team in scoring, assists, and steals, and was second in rebounds.

SCOTTIE PIPPEN

Scottie Pippen has stepped up and replaced Michael Jordan as the Chicago Bulls' go-to player.

Pippen was handed Jordan's mantle, and though a totally different kind of player, he worked to establish a new kind of position – a "point forward" position in which he controls more facets of the game than does any current player. He never worries about how many points he scores and works also to make his teammates better.

Pippen, 6'7", 210 pounds, led the Bulls in scoring, assists and steals, and was second in rebounds during the 1994 season. His 22 points per game average was eighth in the NBA and he hit double figures in each of the 72 games he played. He led Chicago scorers 50 times, and for those games the Bulls were 34-16. His work was recognized by his first-round selection to the NBA's All-League team.

Pippen worked as hard as Jordan ever did, and his effort was rewarded by being chosen by the NBA's coaches to the NBA's All-Defensive team in 1994, for the third year in a row. He got more votes than any other player in the league in this most difficult area of play.

While some pundits made a big deal of Pippen taking himself out of a 1994 playoff game against the Knicks in the final seconds – Chicago won the game – that misstep in no way detracts from the superstar status that he has achieved away from Jordan's mighty shadow.

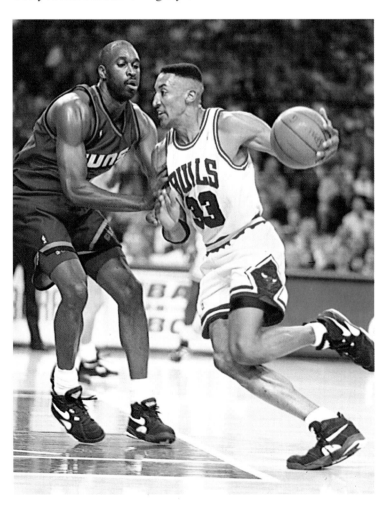

MARK PRICE

Mark Price is the glue that holds the Cleveland Cavaliers together. Over four seasons – from 1991 to 1994 – the Cavaliers were 199-133 with him in the lineup.

The six-foot, 178-pound guard from Georgia Tech skilfully runs Cleveland's offense in the backcourt and he almost single-handedly was responsible for the Cavaliers making the playoffs in 1994 as he led the team in scoring, assists, foul shooting, three-point field goals and steals.

His team scoring title, 17.3 points per game, was his second in his eight NBA seasons. He was high scorer 22 times, and when he scored 20 or more points, Cleveland was 19-12. Price also has become a good three-point field goal shooter, and hit 118 of 297 in 1994. He exhibited that great skill during the NBA's All-Star weekend by winning the Long Distance shooting contest, sinking 20 of 25 shots.

But Price, who was drafted by Dallas on the second round in 1986, truly shines in the backcourt where he is one of the NBA's best point guards. He has led the team in assists six seasons, and he was its assists leader in 61 games during the 1994 season, while averaging nearly eight a game. Cleveland was 23-3 in games in which he had ten or more.

Price leads all active NBA foul shooters with a .906 shooting percentage and has been among the league's top five for six consecutive seasons from 1989.

He played in his fourth All-Star Game in 1994, and scored 20 points; and he was named to Dream Team II that represented the United States in the 1994 World Basketball Championships.

Above and left: Mark Price is one of the NBA's best playmakers, having led his team in assists six times in his first seven seasons; and he also has twice led the Cavaliers in scoring, helped by a top ten finish in five seasons in free throw accuracy and uncanny three-point shooting accuracy.

Opposite: The Miami Heat's most durable player over the past five seasons has been Glen Rice, who once had a 174-consecutive-game streak while becoming the team's all-time scoring leader.

GLEN RICE

Glen Rice of the Miami Heat knows that there is nothing tougher for a talented young rookie player than joining an expansion team and being expected to make it a winner.

But in his first four seasons, the 6'8", 220-pound former Michigan All-America, who was the team's number one pick in the 1990 season accomplished that awesome task.

Rice played a major role in getting the Heat into the playoffs for the first time in 1994 with his best year ever in rebounds, assists and foul shooting; and he had his second best scoring season with a 21.1 average, ranking him among the NBA's top 10.

Rice has had to work his way up to this level of play. He started out averaging just 13.6 points during his rookie season. Now, he keys his team's fortunes. When he scored 20 or more points in 1994, the Heat went 34-12; when he scored less, it went 8-27.

Though Rice led his team in scoring 38 times during that season, he always seemed at his best late in the game. For instance, he scored in double figures 13 times during the fourth quarter.

Rice is a versatile scorer. He was among the NBA foul shooting leaders, and made 130 of 143 over the last 43 games of the 1994 season; and one time, he sank 50 straight foul shots. But he also ranked second among the league's forwards in three-point shooting.

Most of all, he has been very durable and had a streak of 174 consecutive games before the flu forced him to miss a game late in the 1994 season.

MITCH RICHMOND

Mitch Richmond is capable of prodigious feats on the basketball court. A case in point: During the second quarter of a 1994 game between the Sacramento Kings and Philadelphia 76ers, Richmond torched the 76ers for 31 points, 12 rebounds and 10 assists – a triple double in one quarter!

Richmond has averaged nearly 28 points a game since being drafted on the first round by the Golden State Warriors in 1988. He was the NBA's Rookie of the Year and its only unanimous choice on the all-rookie team in 1989. Since 1991, when he was traded to Sacramento, the 6'5", 215-pound guard from Kansas State has been the one shining light for the Kings.

Richmond, the first Sacramento player named to the All-Star team, is on the verge of scoring 10,000 career points. He led the Kings – and was seventh in the NBA – in scoring in 1994 with a 23.4 average, the best by a Kings player in 14 seasons. He has a 116-game streak of having scored 10 or more points in a game, and in 1994 he exceeded 20 points 54 times and 30 points 15 times. He also sank a team record 127 three-point field goals, and had an 8-for-9 night against the L.A. Clippers.

Durability also is his hallmark. He averaged 37.1 minutes per game in 1994, but exceeded 40 minutes in 33 of the 78 games he started.

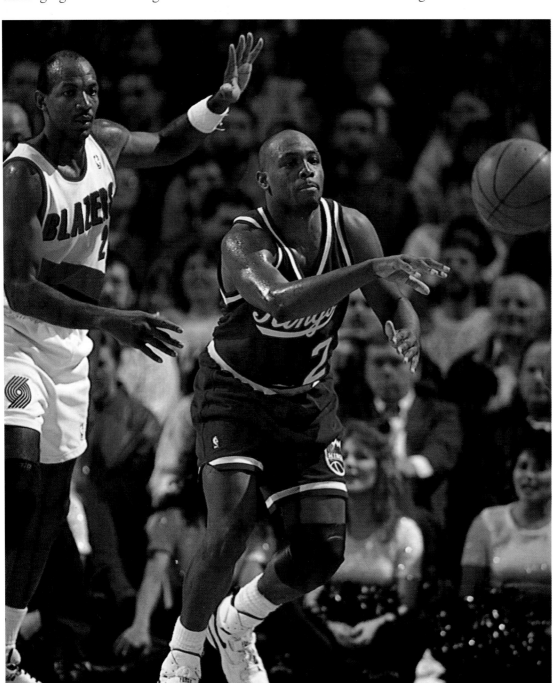

Left: Mitch Richmond not only became the first Sacramento player to appear in an All-Star game, but he also has surpassed the scoring feats of every Kings player since the team moved to Sacramento from Kansas City. In his first six years with the team, he has averaged nearly 23 points per game.

Opposite left: Rik Smits helped to hold opposing center Patrick Ewing to just one point during an Indiana victory in the 1994 Eastern Conference finals.

Opposite right: Smits, a native of Eindhoven, The Netherlands, has been a member of the Dutch National Team since his sophomore year at Maris University in New York.

RIK SMITS

Rik Smits, "the Dunkin' Dutchman" and native of Eindhoven, Holland, came alive during the 1994 season and became the force for the Indiana Pacers that many had long hoped he would be.

Never was this more evident than during the NBA's Eastern Conference final when the 7'4", 265-pound center helped to hold New York Knicks center Patrick Ewing to just one point for an entire game.

Smits took to heart the coaching of Larry Brown and dropped his "soft" game to become more aggressive around the basket. Instead of fadeaway shots, he threw down "in-your-face" dunks; and he began muscling centers for rebounds. He also stopped trying to second-guess his performances by what the statistical sheets said.

"Occasionally after a game I'll look at a boxscore, whereas in the past I got too caught up in the stats," he observed. "Now I just go out and play and don't worry about it."

Brown, who began coaching him in 1994, noted: "In the past, they would go to Rik early and if he didn't score, he'd be pulled and sit. I didn't want him to think he was out there just to score. The points will always come with his abilities. I just had to convince him that we needed him to rebound and play defense, and also that he needed to shed 20 pounds. He did everything we've asked and it got him moving better to take advantage of good athleticism. He's a fine dribbler and passer and he has integrated all of that into his game."

Smits lived up to his coach's expectations in the final month of the 1994 season, when he averaged more than 19 points and eight rebounds a game to help the Pacers into the NBA playoffs.

JOHN STOCKTON

John Stockton, known as "the fastest hands in the West," is the NBA's slickest ballhandler, a veritable magician with the ball.

And contrary to the choir boy image he has been given, there is not a tougher, more hard-nosed player in the NBA. He has missed only four games during his career.

Stockton has accumulated more than 9,300 assists during 10 seasons and is less than 600 from displacing Magic Johnson as the NBA's all-time leader. With more than 2,000 steals, he is less than 200 from passing Maurice Cheeks as the all-time "thief."

"When he clamps on you, he's as mean as they come," said Dennis Rodman of San Antonio, no stranger to rough-house tactics.

"He's got a lot of street in him," notes teammate Karl Malone, with whom he has an almost telepathic playmaking rapport that bedevils opponents.

The 6'1", 175-pound guard has scored 10,000 points during his career; he surpassed 1,000 assists for the sixth time in seven years in 1994; and has led the NBA in assists for seven straight seasons.

Stockton has averaged more than 13 points and 11½ assists per game during his career. Yet, it wasn't until the 1994 season that he was named to the All-NBA first team.

Left: John Stockton of the Utah Jazz streaks past All-Star guard Kevin Johnson of Phoenix with the style that has made him one of the NBA's best all-around guards.

Above: Stockton has been a very durable player, missing only four games during his first ten seasons with the Jazz during which he also was a starter on the All-Star team for five straight seasons.

Opposite left: Dominique Wilkins joined the Los Angeles Clippers in the second half of the 1994 season in a trade with the Atlanta Hawks for Danny Manning.

Opposite right: Wilkins is only the ninth NBA player ever to score 20,000 points. He is among the top five in scoring average.

DOMINIQUE WILKINS

Dominique Wilkins is the consummate NBA superstar.

After blowing out his knee in the early 90s, he worked to reclaim his great talent and team leadership of the Atlanta Hawks; and in 1994, he was en route to one of his best seasons when he was traded to the Los Angeles Clippers for Danny Manning and a number one draft pick. At the end of the 1994 season, he went to the Boston Celtics.

Wilkins, who had played 10 seasons for Atlanta and was well established in the community, then went to the struggling Clippers and did a superb job during the 24 games he played. He led the team in scoring in 19 of them and increased his scoring average five points per game from 24.4 to 29.1 He scored 30 or more points in 13 games with the Clippers (and he did it 26 times with the Hawks), including 34 in his first game and 36 when he returned to Atlanta for the first time to play against his former team.

Wilkins, who started out as a first-round draft pick from the University of Georgia in 1982, ranks second among all active players in scoring with more than 24,000 points – the ninth player in NBA history to reach that plateau. His 26.4 scoring average is tops among all active players.

The 6'8", 215-pound forward has played in eight of the nine All-Star games to which he was named; and he has been selected to the All-NBA team six times.

THE NBA's RISING STARS

Every year, the NBA is infused with a new supply of young talent – tomorrow's pro stars who were yesterday's college heros.

Each of them comes into professional basketball with books of praise-filled press clippings, All-America rankings and gaudy statistics. All of that was richly earned from their college basketball efforts and reflected the many years of working to hone raw skills to bring them to the top of the collegiate level.

Then it starts anew as the players work to succeed at the highest level of competition in the world. Not every one of them will succeed in the same measure because the NBA is a great leveler. They must cope with elements such as luck, meaning primarily remaining injury-free; the caliber of the coaching and talent around them; and their own vitality and perseverance in being willing to work even harder as professionals than they ever worked before.

The NBA, in 1994, welcomed such young stars as Chris Webber, who left the University of Michigan after two All-America seasons and immediately helped to turn around the Golden State Warriors; Anfernee Hardaway, who was the playmaker that Shaquille O'Neal needed to help elevate his game in Orlando; Jamaal Mashburn, who teamed with Jim Jackson, a 1993 rookie, to give the Dallas Mavericks a great young backcourt duo; Isaiah Rider, who starred at UNLV and then had the audacity to warn all the NBA veterans that he would win the NBA's Slam Dunk contest – and he did! And then there was Shawn Bradley, a 7'6" player with limited college experience, but who was willing to broaden his skills in the toughest possible way – while still playing for the Philadelphia 76ers. He wound up as one of the NBA's best upcoming shot-blockers before an injury cut short his rookie season.

Other outstanding talent includes 1993 rookies Ken Anderson of the New Jersey Nets, Golden State's Latrell Sprewell, Philadelphia's Clarence Weatherspoon, and 1992 rookie Larry Johnson, the Hornets' powerful forward.

The cream of this new generation of high achievers comprises the rising stars of the NBA.

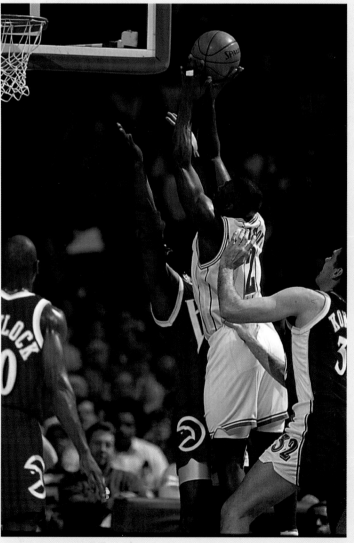

Left: The Minnesota Timberwolves' Isaiah Rider.

Right: 1992 Rookie of the Year Larry Johnson.

KENNY ANDERSON

"If you list the top point guards in the NBA, you must mention his name," said the Knicks' Derek Harper of Kenny Anderson of the New Jersey Nets.

Anderson, who former Nets coach Chuck Daly says "was born to be an NBA point guard," has begun to achieve the star status many predicted of him when he left Georgia Tech after just two seasons to become the Nets' number one draft pick in 1992. In 1994 he was named a starter in the NBA's All-Star Game for the first time en route to completing his first full season as a starter.

Many in the NBA still marvel about his ability to guide his pencil-thin, 6'1", 170-pound frame through NBA traffic with such dexterity. There still were many who questioned the wisdom of the Nets' pick – and Anderson's decision to leave college so early for such a demanding job as point guard – after he lost part of his second season with a fractured wrist. His rookie year was almost a washout because then-Nets coach Bill Fitch used him as a substitute after he had missed training camp because of a contract dispute.

But Anderson began to take charge of the Nets in 1994. He led the team in assists with 784, the fourth best figure in the NBA; was second in scoring for the Nets behind Derrick Coleman, with an 18.8 average; and topped New Jersey with 158 steals.

Right: Kenny Anderson, who was the Nets' Number 1 draft pick in 1991, has recovered from a bumpy start during his first two NBA seasons – a feud with head coach Bill Fitch in his rookie year and a broken wrist after 55 games in his second season – to become an All-Star game starter in his fourth year. He plans on staying at that level, and says, "I study downfalls. I've always wanted to know how a player at the top slips off that pedestal. If I see a guy who had great stats but only made it to one All-Star game, I ask around and find out why. I want to know all the different ways a guy can start to slide so I can avoid them."

SHAWN BRADLEY

Shawn Bradley, a first-round pick of the 76ers in 1993, had limited college playing experience at Brigham Young University because of his mission work. Bradley quickly proved to many in the NBA that he has the potential to be a very fine player – certainly one of the game's best shot blockers.

Until he was forced out of action for the 1994 season after suffering a dislocated left kneecap and chipped bone in a collision with Harvey Grant of the Portland Trail Blazers at midseason, he was getting his NBA feet under him as an impact player of sorts in the middle.

He led the 76ers in blocked shots with 147 in 49 games and pulled down 306 rebounds while also averaging 10.3 points per game. He had five double-doubles; in seven games he blocked seven or more shots; and he exhibited flashes of scoring while still the rawest of rookies. He was chosen on the second All-NBA rookie team.

However, his biggest obstacle to becoming an all-out force is himself – or precisely, his ability to add some girth to his 7′6″ frame. He weighs a stringbean (for him) 235 pounds, but finds it very hard to add weight; and when he does, to keep it on. However, he was unafraid to throw himself around against big, physical centers – as his numbers indicate.

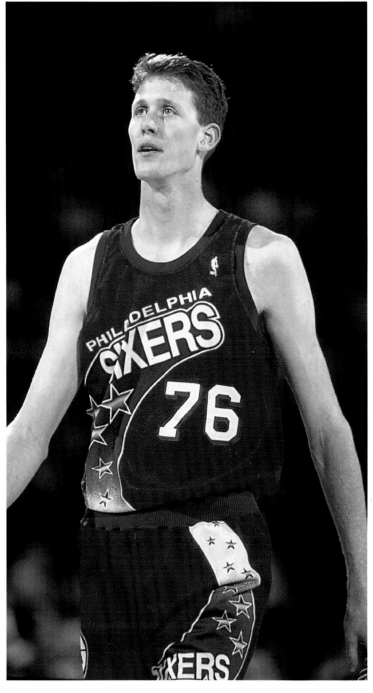

ANFERNEE HARDAWAY

Anfernee Hardaway was the NBA's 24-carat gold rookie in 1994, the only one to start all 82 games. As a member of the Orlando Magic he averaged more than 36 minutes a game. He also was tied with Golden State's Chris Webber for most votes for the 1994 NBA All-Rookie team.

Ironically, Hardaway, a 6′7″ guard from Memphis State, came to Orlando in a 1993 draft day trade with the Golden State Warriors for Webber after the Magic had made the Michigan All-America the draft's first selection.

Leading all rookies in assists and steals, and ranking fourth in scoring, Hardaway helped lead the Magic to its winningest season.

Hardaway added a solid backcourt dimension to go with super center Shaquille O'Neal. He played both the point guard and shooting guard position during the season and led the Magic in assists with nearly seven per game, including a season high 15 against Golden State. He also was 14th in the NBA in assists, remarkable for a rookie.

Hardaway also added immediate offense as the Magic's number two scorer behind O'Neal with 16 points per game, and he showed an immediate talent for defense as he failed to get a steal in only eight games, finishing with 190, sixth best in the NBA. He had five steals in a game three times and four in 17 other games.

Opposite left: Shawn Bradley uses his seven-and-a-half feet to stuff a lay-up by the Knicks' John Starks, displaying the talent that prompted the Philadelphia 76ers to make him a Number 1 draft pick in 1994.

Opposite right: Bradley had little playing experience at Brigham Young because he spent two years on required missionary work. But he has been tutored by two former great NBA centers — Moses Malone and Kareem Abdul-Jabbar — and has showed flashes of potential greatness during his rookie season. His biggest problem is gaining more weight and maintaining it.

Right: Anfernee Hardaway helped to rev up the Orlando Magic's offense and propel it to the playoffs for the first time in 1994 when he gave center Shaquille O'Neal some needed backcourt help.

LARRY JOHNSON

Larry Johnson proved during his brilliant rookie season in 1992 that he could be one of the NBA's top performers. Now he is on another mission to prove that his injury-plagued third year in 1994 was an aberration and that he is indeed headed for the top echelon among the NBA's stars.

Johnson suffered a lower back spasm that cost him 31 games during the 1994 season, and the Hornets were 9-22 during his absence, costing them a second straight playoff appearance. He helped them to a 32-19 record when he played, and when he returned for the final 25 games, the team was 17-8.

Johnson, a 6'7" 250-pound forward, is a small but power-ful front court player for whom durability had never been a problem. In his first two seasons, he played every game and led the NBA in minutes played. He had the NBA's third longest consecutive game playing streak at 184 games when his injury forced him to the bench.

Johnson scored in double figures in 16 of his final 17 games in 1994 and there is every indication that he will play back to the form that made him the team's first NBA All-Star Game participant in 1993 and a unanimous Rookie of the Year selection in 1992. He was selected to play on Dream Team II in the World Basketball Championships in 1994.

Left: Larry Johnson of the Charlotte Hornets makes one of his patented stuff shots. Though considered a "small" forward at 6' 7", Johnson is incredibly strong and quick and can match up against bigger players.

Opposite: Jamaal Mashburn's 19-point scoring average led every NBA rookie during his first season (1994), and he teamed well with another young guard, Jim Jackson, to give the Dallas Mavericks a solid backcourt combination.

JAMAAL MASHBURN

Former Nets coach Chuck Daly minced few words when he talked about the rookie season of Dallas Mavericks forward Jamaal Mashburn: "He reminds me of (Larry) Bird. He's a passer who has a post-up game and an outside game. . . . He has a chance to be a premier player in the game."

Mashburn, a first-round pick of the Mavericks, proved it with his 19.2 scoring average, best of all NBA rookies in '94, and by playing on the NBA's All-Rookie first team.

He and guard Jim Jackson are the bright hopes for the Mavericks. They teamed to score 50 or more points nine times during Mashburn's first season and they also had 60 in a losing game against Orlando.

In becoming the first Mavericks player to surpass 1,000 points in a season since Sam Perkins in 1989, Mashburn, a 6'8", 240-pound forward from the University of Kentucky, led his team in scoring 37 times. He was first in team rebounds 13 times; and he led the Mavs in assists 16 times. Mashburn hit double figures in scoring in 73 of the 79 games in which he played; and he had 37 20-point games and seven 30-point efforts.

"He's already one of the young stars of the NBA," said Charlotte coach Allan Bristow. "He has a nice inside game and can put the ball on the floor as well. He's got a lot of weapons."

ISAIAH RIDER

Isaiah Rider was born to play in a city like New Orleans with all of its splash and glitter (if the Minnesota Timberwolves ever make good on their intention to move there).

Rider proved during his rookie 1993 season with the Minnesota Timberwolves that he fits that profile. His flamboyant streak was evident from the first, when on draft day he promised that he would win the NBA's Slam Dunk contest during the All-Star weekend. Backing up his words with action, he pulled off a thrilling "East Bay Funk Dunk" that made him the new kind of slam against a field of veterans.

The 6'5" Rider plays a very up-tempo game and may remind New Orleans of Pete Maravich, who played for the Jazz during its existence in the Crescent City. Maravich was its leader in scoring, steals and assists, and played at a frenetic pace with his constant movement, no-look passes and fancy dribbling, complete with flying hair and droopy socks, that made him a cult hero.

Rider, an All-America when at UNLV, plays at the same pace when he heads for the basket. He averaged 16.6 points a game for the Timberwolves in 1994, and had four rebounds and nearly three assists per game. He ranked third among all NBA rookie scorers, and he was the fifth best vote-getter on the NBA's All-Rookie team.

Left: Isaiah Rider of the Minnesota Timberwolves slams home one of his dunks while winning the NBA's 1994 Slam Dunk competition – a feat that he predicted for himself even before he signed his first NBA contract.

Opposite left and right: Latrell Sprewell was the 24th player picked on the first round of the 1992 draft – not a spot that inspires visions of stardom – but the former Alabama All-America became the youngest player in 15 seasons to lead Golden State in scoring. In 1994, he became the first player since Detroit's Bill Laimbeer in 1983 to participate in an All-Star game though his name was left off the fans' ballots.

LATRELL SPREWELL

At first it was "Latrell Who?" Now is it "Latrell – Wow!"

Latrell Sprewell (prounounced SPREE-well), a 6'5", 190-pound guard from Alabama, was Golden State's first-round pick in 1992, and only devoted NBA draftniks really knew about him.

No longer.

Sprewell has taken the NBA by storm. After his second season in 1994, he was named to the All-NBA first team; he was selected by the coaches to fill a spot in the All-Star Game midway through that season; and he began rewriting the Golden State record book.

Most of all, Sprewell is indefatigable. He set a record at Alabama for minutes played and he has led the Warriors in playing time in his first two seasons. In 1994 he played 3,533 minutes (43.1 per game), or the equivalent of more than 73½ regulation games of an 82-game season!

"The guy is just tireless," says Golden State coach Don Nelson. "The amazing thing is that he's got just as much energy in the 40th minute as he does in the first."

In 1994 the 23-year-old Sprewell was the youngest Warriors player ever to lead the team in scoring since 1980, with a 21.0 average. He led the team in scoring in 43 games; set a club record with 141 three-point field goals; was tops with 180 steals; and was second with 385 assists.

CLARENCE WEATHERSPOON

Nothing seems to faze Clarence Weatherspoon – after all, he is the youngest of 13 children. And he certainly displayed that cool during his first two seasons with the Philadelphia 76ers when he started every game and played with poise that startled many NBA veterans.

Weatherspoon was a number one draft pick in 1992 from Southern Mississippi, where he was only the second athlete ever to have his jersey retired. (Former Oakland Raiders punter Ray Guy was the other.)

The 6′6″, 245-pound forward had an immediate impact on the 76ers. He set a team rookie scoring record with 1,280 points and showed that he "plays big." In 1993 Weatherspoon had 17 games with 20 or more points; 19 games with 10 or more rebounds; and he led the Sixers with 18 double-doubles. He was second in the NBA's Slam Dunk Contest during his rookie year.

During his first two seasons he led his team in rebounds, averaging 7.2 per game in 1993 and 10.1 in 1994. He also topped the 76ers in scoring in 1994 with 18.4 points per game, and was second in steals (100) and blocked shots (11.6). He hit 45 double-doubles, eighth highest in team history. Weatherspoon scored a career-high 31 points against Cleveland, and a month later he pulled down a career-best 23 rebounds battling Shaquille O'Neal of Orlando.

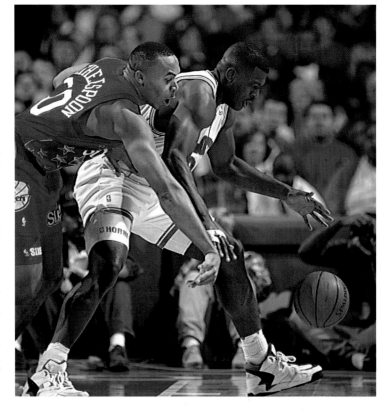

hadn't won the honor once during his freshman year.

He made the All-America team as a sophomore and was also chosen National Player of the Year by *The Sporting News* after averaging 20 points per game.

Smith then ordered Michael to work on his ballhandling skills and he repeated as a unanimous All-America player in his junior season. He led the ACC with a 19.7 scoring average, finishing the year with 1,788 points, ninth best in North Carolina history.

Opposite: Jordan was a two-time All-America player at the University of North Carolina, and twice was selected as College Player of the Year. As a freshman in 1992, he sank the game-winning basket that gave the Tar Heels the NCAA title.

Right: Jordan was a Number 1 pick of the Chicago Bulls in 1984 – a choice they had not planned on making because personnel director Jerry Krause favored center Sam Bowie of Kentucky, who was taken a pick ahead of Jordan.

The Greatest of All Bulls

Michael Jordan was the "luckiest" number one draft pick the Chicago Bulls ever made. They had the third pick in the first round of the 1984 draft and Chicago general manager Jerry Krause coveted Kentucky's 7'1" center Sam Bowie, despite the fact that Jordan had been acclaimed the best player in college basketball; he was forgoing his senior year at North Carolina; and he was heading for the Olympics with one of the most talented U.S. teams ever.

Left: Jordan displays the second of three NBA Most Valuable Player awards that he won, this one in 1991 when he led the Chicago Bulls to their best record ever en route to winning their first NBA title.

Opposite: Jordan drives past James Worthy and Hakeem Olajuwon of the West team for two of the team-leading 19 points that he scored in the 1990 NBA All-Star Game, one of nine in which he appeared. He was MVP in the 1988 game.

When Portland picked Bowie with the second pick, Krause was "forced" to take Jordan.

How did it turn out?

- Three consecutive NBA titles
- Three NBA MVP Awards
- Three NBA Playoff MVP Awards
- Seven straight NBA scoring titles
- Nine All-Star Game appearances
- A lifetime's worth of astounding plays

Michael was special from the start. He signed a record five-year, $4 million contract, the highest at that time for any guard – rookie or veteran – in NBA history. Within three seasons, the Bulls had broken all previous attendance records; their TV audience expanded to record proportions; and Jordan's effect was such that one-third of the NBA's increased attendance came from Bulls games.

He led the NBA in scoring with 2,313 points; helped Chicago to a playoff berth and 11 more victories than the previous season; and was selected Rookie of the Year.

Even as a rookie, he caused Krause to grumble that "he's such a great competitor, even in practice, that he tends to dominate his own teammates and that can, at times, disrupt practice in the same way he disrupts opponents during a game."

Still, he went through an adjustment period but he didn't allow the pressure to bother him.

"At Carolina, I played in a controlled system, and a lot of the crowd was pleased with my play," he said. "In the NBA, when I played my natural game, I didn't have any problems with the crowd. Actually, it was the most relaxed time of my career to that point because, while there were more games, they came so quickly that if I had a bad one, I could quickly put the past behind me and get ready for the present."

This very practical approach was pure Michael Jordan – prepared for any eventuality. For example, in high school, believing that he would forever be a bachelor, he took a course in home economics; at North Carolina, and facing more media attention, he took a media course so he could better understand the demands.

His second NBA season was only three games old when he broke a bone in his foot and sat out 64 games. The inactivity gnawcd at him. Returning to North Carolina to take courses toward his degree, he played pick-up basketball games when he felt his foot had healed. The doctors had wanted him to sit out the entire season but he refused and they reluctantly agreed that he could play in the last 15 games. The result? He averaged 22.7 points and literally carried the Bulls back into the playoffs.

In those playoffs, he staged one of the most spectacular performances of his career: a record-setting, 63-point, double overtime performance against Larry Bird and the Boston Celtics, and he broke the mark in typical Jordan fashion – with a swooping, soaring drive over Celtics seven-foot center Robert Parish.

Record-breaking became commonplace with Jordan. In 1987 he scored 50 points against the New York Knicks, the most ever by a visiting player in New York, remarkable considering the great players who had come through that city during the 40 years of the NBA's existence. But Michael always elevated his game against the great players and teams, particularly if challenged.

In addition to his competitiveness with Bird, two of Michael's earliest rivalries were against the Laker's Magic Johnson and Isiah Thomas of the Detroit Pistons. When he made the NBA All-Star team in his rookie season, Thomas, with Magic Johnson's approval, didn't get Jordan the ball when the two of them were in the game together. Michael found out about that plot and he never forgot the slight, even snubbing a coveted berth in Johnson's annual, post-season all-star game for many years. He got his revenge in 1991 when the Bulls first eliminated the two-time NBA champion Pistons in four straight games in the Eastern Conference finals; and then took out Johnson and the Lakers in five games to win their first NBA title.

In every one of his seasons with Chicago, he was the absolute team leader on and off the court. He seemed to

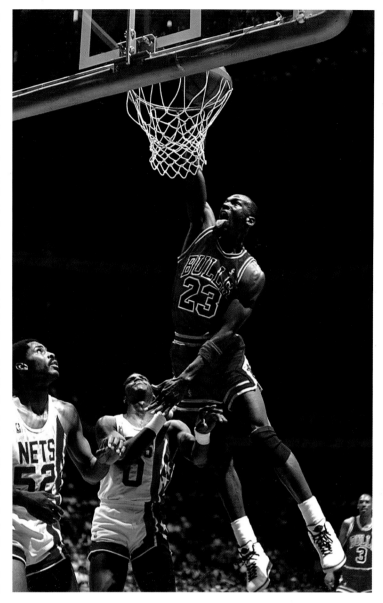

Opposite: The classic "inside" Michael Jordan move – tongue sticking out while maneuvering between defenders (this time, those of the Seattle Supersonics) – to score a basket.

Above right: The classic "outside" Michael Jordan maneuver – tongue extended and a virtual sky walk to score a basket.

Right: Jordan with East coach K.C. Jones of the Boston Celtics in his first NBA All-Star Game, during his 1985 rookie season.

delight in working over his teammates in practice, but it was only to try and make them better. For the first several years in Chicago, he openly feuded with Krause about the lack of a superior supporting cast. It wasn't until Chicago added Scottie Pippen, Horace Grant and Bill Cartwright to go with John Paxson and Jordan in the late eighties that the Bulls finally became serious title contenders and Jordan felt comfortable with the players around him.

No one could shut him down. Even Michael Cooper of the Lakers, one of the NBA's premier defensive players during the eighties and always credited with doing the best job against him, noted wryly: "When people say that I, or some other player, shut him down, that's wrong. I need the whole team and so does every other player who takes him on. As soon as he touches the ball . . . you don't know what he's going to do. He goes right, left, over you, around and under you. He twists, he turns. And you know he's going to get the shot off. You just don't know when and how . . . the most devastating thing psychologically to a defender."

The most underrated part of Jordan's game was his defense. He made the league's all-defensive team six consecutive years; and he often said he got more satisfaction making great defensive plays than in leading all scorers. In 1988 he was selected as Defensive Player of the Year. Johnny Bach, the Bulls' defensive coach, said he was "like all the furies of hell unleashed" when he went out to shut down a rival scorer. "In the final two minutes of a close game, we often put him against the opposition's best scorer, regardless of size or position," Bach said, "and it was just awesome to watch Michael go to work. He was like a Tasmanian Devil."

Jordan's quickness and ability to anticipate are evident in the fact that he was always among the leaders in steals. In 1987 he was the first player ever to get more than 200 in one season (236). His 125 blocked shots that year were the most ever by a guard. The following year he broke that record with 131.

He played the first five seasons as the Bulls' "off" or shooting guard, but midway through the 1988 season, he agreed to shift to the "point guard" position where he would control the offense. Many criticized the move but he quickly silenced them when, over a span of 10 straight games, he notched triple-doubles – double figures in scoring, rebounding and assists.

Above: Few players in NBA history held as many scoring records as Jordan, who was a veritable scoring machine from anyplace on the court.

Left: Jordan teamed with Scottie Pippen (right) to form a fearsome one-two scoring and defensive punch during the Bulls' championship seasons.

Opposite: Air Jordan at his finest – when he brought skywalking a new dimension in pro basketball for nine seasons.

From that point until his retirement, he was the best point guard in the NBA. He energized himself and his mates with his playmaking and scoring. "It was a challenge that I enjoyed," he said, "because the point guard's job is to distribute the ball, to be a leader . . . to be like another coach on the floor. That's what I wanted to do even though I had played the off-guard position all my life and its really my natural position."

With his competitive spirit, Jordan really shone in the playoffs. The Bulls would have won four in a row had not Jordan injured his foot in the opening game of the 1990 playoffs and was sub-par while Detroit won the Eastern Conference Finals in seven games.

In 1991 the Bulls dispatched the Lakers in five games, capping a sensational season during which Jordan scored his 15,000th career point, and scored 30 or more points 52 times. The Bulls lost the first game of the Finals, then ran off four straight wins, the last in which Jordan started the game with a small hole in his sneaker to alleviate some of the pressure on a mashed little right toe. He didn't like the feel, and went back to his regular Air Jordans, then scored or assisted on seven of Chicago's first 10 second-half field goals. He artfully directed a fourth-quarter attack by feeding Scottie Pippen, who scored 32 points, and then Paxson, who threw in a succession of three-point shots, en route to a 108-101 victory.

The following year, Jordan led the Bulls to their second straight world title as the Bulls beat the Portland Trail Blazers in six games. In 1993 after starring with America's Dream Team in the 1992 Olympic Games, he charged up the Bulls for a run at their third straight title. Many believe this was Jordan's finest season because it was as if he willed

Left: It never seemed to matter whether Jordan was outnumbered or not, as he was here in the 1988 All-Star game, because he scored two of his 40 points en route to winning the game's MVP Award.

Opposite top left: One of Jordan's most remarkable achievements was leading the Bulls from an 0-2 deficit against the New York Knicks and winning four straight games for the Eastern Conference title in 1993.

Opposite top right: Head-to-head with Phoenix's Dan Majerle in the 1993 NBA Finals.

Opposite below: How sweet it was for Jordan, who cradles the Bulls' second NBA championship trophy in 1992.

the team to a title with his own efforts. "If not for Michael, no title," said Johnny Bach. "There is no doubt that he literally carried us when it sometimes seemed we didn't want to be carried."

Jordan averaged nearly 40 minutes a game during the regular season but shrugged off the mental and physical fatigue that had dogged him throughout the season, and averaged more than 45 minutes in the 19 playoff games. He climaxed a four-game sweep of Cleveland by scoring the winning basket at the buzzer; he brought the Bulls back from an 0-2 deficit against New York in the Eastern Conference Finals with a 54-point performance to help even the series at 2-2; and then he had 29- and 25-point games to complete the Bulls' four-in-a-row streak for the conference title.

In the NBA Finals against Phoenix, Jordan scored 40 or more points in five of the six games, including 55 in a 111-105 victory in Game 5. He snuffed out any Suns player with a hot scoring hand. When Dan Majerle scored six three-point field goals for Phoenix in the third game and two more at the end of the first half in Game 4, Jordan took over and held him to two meaningless two-point field goals as Chicago won the game.

In Game 6, Chicago went six minutes without a field goal in the last quarter and blew an eight-point lead. During a timeout, Jordan told his teammates he would take care of the scoring – and he scored Chicago's next 12 points, the last two on an end-to-end run that cut Phoenix' lead to two points with 40 seconds to play.

He then stepped up on defense and forced Phoenix to re-linquish the ball without taking a shot. When Chicago took the ball, he started the play that produced Paxson's winning three-point basket in a 99-98 victory, then added one final defensive touch when he forced a desperate, no-chance, last-second shot by Kevin Johnson that was blocked by Horace Grant.

That series, in which he averaged 41 points per game, plus nine rebounds and seven assists, and the clinching game – in which he had 33 points, eight rebounds and a team-high seven assists in 44 minutes of play, were the finest of his career.

With all of that came the tragedy of his father's death after the 1993 season. Michael and his father were more like brothers than like father and son during the first few years of Michael's career because they went everywhere together when the team was on the road. "His death left a huge void in Michael's life and made him realize just how temporary everything really is," a friend said. "It obvious-ly moved him to reassess his own life in regards to his im-mediate family (wife and two children) and he felt it was up to him to reestablish his entire family."

Just as the Bulls were preparing to open training camp for 1994, Jordan stunned the world by announcing his re-tirement though he left one glimmer of hope that he might some day return to the NBA when he commented, "I never say never to anything."

Opposite: The final exit? Jordan goes whooping off the court after leading the Bulls to the title-clinching victory for their third straight NBA championship in 1993 – the last game he played before announcing his retirement a few months later.

Above: Jordan and his "best friend" – his father James, whose tragic death in 1993 profoundly changed Jordan's life and hastened his decision to retire.

Right: Jordan embraces rival Charles Barkley of the Phoenix Suns after his team defeated the Suns for the 1993 NBA title. Both had been teammates on the 1992 U.S. Olympic gold medal team.

A Double Gold Performance

In 1984 Indiana's Bobby Knight was named head coach of the U.S. team in the Los Angeles Olympic Games. He knew there would be tremendous pressure to produce a team that could win in front of the home folks, so he put out a call to every good college basketball player to come to a series of tryouts he was holding in the late spring to choose a team.

Michael Jordan answered the call.

In his final pre-NBA hurrah, he joined an Olympic team of such collegiate stars as Patrick Ewing, Alvin Robertson, Chris Mullin, Wayman Tisdale, Sam Perkins and Steve Alford – and he helped the team win all eight of its games while averaging 17 points per game.

He thrived under Knight's demand for a wide open offensive game, and a vise-like defense to offset the more

MICHAEL JORDAN

Left: There was no doubt who was the most recognizable star of the 1992 Olympic Games in Barcelona, Spain. Jordan was part of the U.S. Dream Team comprised of 11 NBA players and one collegian.

Opposite top: Jordan wears the net from the U.S. basket as a symbol of victory after his team won the gold medal in the 1984 Olympics.

Opposite below: Part of the U.S. 1992 Dream Team: Scottie Pippen (left), Jordan's Chicago Bulls teammate; Jordan; and Clyde Drexler of the Portland Trail Blazers.

liberal international rules under which the Games are played.

The team won the gold medal by an average of 32 points a game, and Jordan led all scorers. In the clinching game against Spain, he led the U.S. team with 30 points. With his gold medal locked safely away, Jordan thought that phase of his career was over, but eight years later he would again answer the call.

For years, teams from nations other than the U.S. used professional players, including many from the NBA, in international competition and the Olympics. The collegiate-dominated U.S. teams were more and more at a disadvantage until the U.S. Olympic Committee decided that it would open its squad to any U.S. player – including NBA stars.

Thus was born the 1992 Dream Team, and 11 of its 12 players were NBA stars. Of course, star number 1 was Jordan, who had just led the Bulls to their second straight NBA title. He was teamed in the backcourt with Magic Johnson, recently retired from the NBA. The Dream

Team included such stars as Patrick Ewing and Chris Mullin from the 1984 team; Michael's teammate Scottie Pippen; Larry Bird, who had just played his final NBA season; Utah's Karl Malone and John Stockton; Clyde Drexler, whose Trail Blazers had just lost to Jordan and the Bulls in the 1992 NBA Finals; and Charles Barkley.

Jordan, the world's most renowned athlete, easily could have dominated the scene. But he fitted himself into coach Chuck Daly's star-studded lineup and was a consistent contributor as the U.S. easily swept to another gold medal.

It was easily the best show in Barcelona. When Johnson ran the offense, Jordan would finish off Magic's radar-like passes with his soaring, swooping style of play; when Michael ran the offense, it was less flamboyant but spiced with some no-look passes to other players cutting toward the basket for easy shots.

When Daly wanted to shut down the opposing star, he turned to Jordan. He smothered Sarunas Marciulionis of Lithuania, against whom he had played in the NBA, in a key semifinal game; and repeated the feat against future Chicago Bull Tony Kukoc when the U.S. defeated Croatia for the gold medal. He also topped all scorers in that game with 22 points.

Michael and the Grand Old Game

Like any other kid when he was growing up, Michael Jordan dreamed of becoming a major league baseball star. Baseball was his first love until he discovered basketball.

Even then, he pursued it as a fine player at Laney High School in his hometown of Wilmington, North Carolina.

But he could not pursue a two-sport career at North Carolina because basketball consumed more than half the school year. So Michael put his baseball dream aside until he began visiting Chicago's Comiskey Park during the winter of 1994 after his retirement from the NBA and saw the batting machines being used by many of the players in their off-season drills.

Those dreams of being a major leaguer quickly resurfaced – along with the challenge of competition that still burned so hotly within him – and he purchased some bats to take regular cuts against the machines. Soon thereafter, he convinced White Sox owner Jerry Reinsdorf, who also owned the Bulls and was a close friend, to sign him to a contract. Thus was born, in the spring of 1994, Michael Jordan, major league prospect. He had not played since high school and at age 31 when many major league players were beginning to wind down their careers, Michael was attempting to start one

At the White Sox training site in Florida, he attracted more attention than anyone in the major leagues – and he had never even played a professional game! Every swing, every catch, every throw was photographed, written about and discussed – sometimes with bitterness by the sport's self-styled purists and even some players who resented anyone without "credentials" daring to master the Grand Old Game.

Opposite: Jordan was able to give his childhood passion for baseball the ultimate test when he signed a contract with the Chicago White Sox after he had retired from the Bulls. It was a longshot because he had not played the sport since his high school days and after working out in spring training, he was sent to the Sox's minor league team in Birmingham, Alabama, where he struggled to maintain a .200 average.

Right: Whether it was scoring a basket or throwing a baseball, Jordan's tongue always came into play.

Michael's job wasn't easy because he was starting from scratch with only his great athletic ability and work ethic to fuel his pursuit. No one ever worked harder and if nothing else, he was a wonderful role model to young players trying to forge a career – and to those older ones who cared to watch and learn.

Still, it was obvious that he needed time in the minor leagues and he started the 1994 season at Birmingham. In a class move he purchased a luxury bus, complete with on-board TV sets, for his team's road games.

The odds were always long for him becoming a major league player – not only because of his talent and age, but also because he may not have the patience to endure much time in the minor leagues. He is competing in a grind that taxes players many years younger, who are sustained only by their dreams of becoming a star – a star of Michael Jordan's magnitude.

Michael, the Mogul

There has never been a more successful business athlete than Michael Jordan. In the first 10 years of his professional career, he realized over $100 million from endorsements of such varied products as shoes, hamburgers, soft drinks, clothes, sporting goods and breakfast cereals.

In 1993, his last season in the NBA, he earned at least $28 million from endorsing products, more than eight times his basketball salary. In 1994, even though he relegated himself to pursuing a baseball career in the minor leagues, the Nike Shoe Company realized $200 million in sales from their line of Air Jordan sneakers – and he wasn't even playing basketball!

Jordan's wonderfully entertaining commercials with an-

Above: Jordan was as big a star away from the basketball court as he was on it with millions of dollars worth of product endorsements and some show biz deals such as an appearance on the popular "Saturday Night Live" television show, where he posed with the cast.

Left: Jordan was involved in his baseball career at a time when many major league players have passed the peak of their careers.

Opposite: Jordan's popularity among American sports stars was unparalleled during the last part of his NBA career.

other former NBA star and endorsement giant, Larry Bird, for McDonald's restaurants – "off the roof, through the window, off the backboard . . . nothing but net" – were award winners for both the client and the athlete.

Jordan rang up big numbers from the time he signed his first NBA contract in 1984 and even before he had swooped in for his first layup when Nike introduced its Air Jordan sneakers. No one knew he would emerge as such a great star, but some creative marketing by the ProServe Agency that handled his contract started him on a career that has made him one of sports' most successful endorsement stars.

Jordan turned every commercial venture into a profit. Autographed basketballs go for $600 each, and auto-graphed baseballs bring $300, though he is only a minor leaguer.

Though Michael's NBA career may be over and a base-ball career strictly an iffy thing, his endorsement career continues as companies alter their advertising strategy to reflect a different image than the successful on-the-court persona.

Unlike most athletes involved with product endorse-ments, Jordan maintains active involvement in the de-cision-making processes that accompany all endorsement strategies. He is very comfortable in the board room per-haps because the competitive aspects of the business world are not so different from those of the athletic world – and even more lucrative.

THE ULTIMATE RIVALRIES

Matchup: Two men competing against each other. It is the essence of such individual sports as tennis, boxing and wrestling but a rarity in team-oriented sports, except baseball were the game really focuses on the contest between pitcher and hitter.

But every so often, that coveted contest of wills and abilities pops up in a team sport such as basketball – as it did during the sixties in the NBA when the two greatest centers of all time, Bill Russell and Wilt Chamberlain, battled each other – and during the eighties when Magic Johnson and Larry Bird brought their teams into combat against each other.

Because Bird and Johnson did not really go one-on-one on every play, their personal competition never reached the proportions of the Russell-Chamberlain duels. In the sixties the centers were the dominant players on the court, and everything revolved around their actions.

Above and left: Larry Bird (left) and Magic Johnson (above) began their classic rivalry in college, when Bird played for Indiana State and Johnson played for Michigan State. They carried it into the NBA, where they made Celtics-Lakers games truly memorable throughout the 1980s.

WILT CHAMBERLAIN VS. BILL RUSSELL

Bill Russell changed the way offenses were grouped around a center after he joined the Celtics during the 1957 season. Until then, dominating centers like George Mikan and Neil Johnston had primarily been scorers whose size against smaller players also gave them a rebounding edge.

Russell, who was 6'10", brought to the game an athleticism never before seen in a big man. He played the defensive role at the insistence of coach Red Auerbach who told him, "Never mind scoring, just get me the ball. I've got plenty of guys who can score."

He did it better than any player in the game's history. He could outjump men taller than him; he was quicker than smaller forwards and guards; and he used his physical talents to force opposing offenses away from the basket.

Shot-blocking was not entirely new, but Russell really made it an art form because he not only blocked the shot, he usually kept the ball in play for himself or directed it to a teammate to trigger the Celtics' devastating fast-break offense.

But his dominance was challenged when Wilt Chamberlain entered the NBA in the 1960 season.

Chamberlain was truly a phenomenal physical specimen – 7'1" and 265 pounds, and one of the greatest athletes ever to play any sport.

Chamberlain was more offensive-minded than Russell. When he came into the NBA in the 1960 season, his great strength and offensive skills were expected to negate Russell's great defense. Chamberlain's scoring achievements tell the story of his abilities. Wilt still is the only player ever to score 100 points in an NBA game; he won the

Above right: Bill Russell led the University of San Francisco to back-to-back NCAA titles in 1955-56, and then polished off his college career by being named MVP in the East-West College All-Star game.

Right: Wilt Chamberlain followed Bill Russell as college basketball's dominating center when he was selected to the All-America team as a sophomore in 1957 while leading his Kansas Jayhawks into the NCAA Final Four.

scoring title in his first seven seasons; and he finished his career with a 30.1 points per game average, second only to Michael Jordan.

Always overlooked, though, was his ability to challenge Russell's rebounding strength. Wilt led the NBA in rebounding for eight of the 10 seasons he and Russell competed against each other. In the end, though, Russell had the ultimate edge: He won world championships in nine of the 10 years he played against Chamberlain.

When they faced each other, everyone in the NBA seemed to stand aside and watch. The only time Boston Garden was filled in those years was when Wilt came to town, and when the Celtics reached the NBA Finals.

The first time the two titans faced each other was on November 7, 1959, in Boston Garden. Russell, then beginning his third NBA season, had 22 points and 35 rebounds while Chamberlain, a rookie, had 30 points and 28 rebounds. That game set the standard for every encounter until Russell retired after the 1969 season.

Russell's memory of that game was vivid.

"Both of us grabbed a loose ball at the same time and I tried to yank it away from him," he recalled. "Did you ever try to bend a lamp post with your bare hands? That's how strong Wilt's arms were.

"Then he began to pull on me. I actually felt my feet leaving the floor, and I thought, 'I'm going to look awful silly if he stuffs the ball and me through the hoop.'

Above: Bill Russell was named to the NBA All-Star team for 12 of his 13 NBA seasons and he was chosen MVP in the 1963 game, thanks to a 24-rebound performance.

Left: Russell vs. Chamberlain in 1960, the first season they began their head-to-head confrontation.

Opposite above and below: Wilt Chamberlain was often an unstoppable force – even against rival Bill Russell, who gave away three inches to his rival. Part of Russell's game plan against Wilt the Stilt was to make his shot selection as difficult as possible by keeping him away from his favorite spot near the basket.

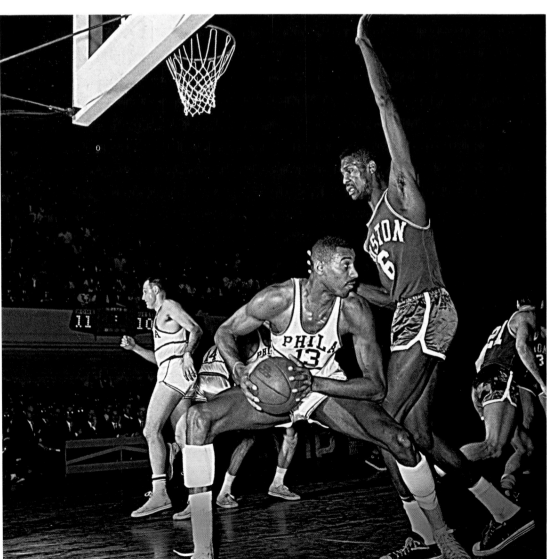

"Fortunately, the referee blew the whistle for a jump ball."

Almost 10 years later they repeated the same scene during the seventh game of the 1968 Eastern Conference finals. Each had a vise-like grip on the ball but in making one final effort to secure it for himself Wilt lifted Russell, still clutching the ball, in the air and spun him completely around. Russell never let go.

Their rivalry was portrayed as good vs. bad almost from the start, often presented in the media as the classic match between a boxer (Russell) and a puncher (Chamberlain), brains against brawn, teamwork against individual enterprise. The good guy (Russell) triumphed in the end. They faced each other 98 times during their 10 years of regular season competition, and Russell held a 57-41 edge; they met in eight playoffs and Russell's edge was 29-20. Wilt, who played against Russell as a member of the Philadelphia Warriors, San Francisco Warriors, Philadelphia 76ers and Los Angeles Lakers, won only in 1967 when the 76ers eliminated the Celtics in five games, then went on to win the NBA title.

"The rivalry between them was so intense that it ran into the off-season," says John Havlicek, who played with Russell for seven seasons. "Russell waited for Wilt to sign his contract and then he'd ask for one dollar more."

That happened in 1965 when Chamberlain became the first NBA player ever to get a $100,000 per year salary. A

couple of days later, Russell signed with Boston for $100,001.

Russell's game was as much mental as it was physical because he knew that no one ever could overwhelm Chamberlain in a pure physical battle. There was a mutual respect off the court, but a fierce intensity on the court that never erupted into any personal extracurricular combat.

In fact, Russell, in his first autobiography, *Go Up For Glory*, recalled they came close only once: "Perhaps the closest we ever came was [that] memorable incident in 1964 in Boston when Auerbach came running up from the bench and started an argument with Wilt at midcourt.

"For years we all wondered what would happen if Wilt ever got mad. We figured it was a case of just running out of the hall because Chamberlain just has to be the strongest man alive . . .

"In this particular game, Wilt wasn't cooling off. He had just plain and simply had enough, between transferring to San Francisco and getting a lot of bad raps and one thing and another. Then Red came up to exchange remarks.

"Red was within four feet of Wilt on the sidelines as I ran up. I put my hand out on Wilt's arm and yelled, 'Get back, Red, you're six inches too close.'

"Auerbach, yelling all the while, took one giant step back and at the same time, Chamberlain just shook off my hand with one sweep.

"I thought, 'Okay Wilt, if that's the way you feel, then go ahead.'"

At that moment, fate in the person of Russell's teammate Clyde Lovelette intervened and when he threatened to take a poke at Wilt, Chamberlain decked him with a flick of his huge right hand.

"We found out what we wanted to know – Chamberlain can hit," Russell wrote. The two never came close to combat again but there was always a tremendous intensity to their on-court contests that sometimes were spiced by glares, growls, a few heated words and an occasional shove.

Russell and Chamberlain often socialized together, though former Celtics publicist Howie McHugh once

Left: Despite a solid 15-point career scoring average Russell was never as renowned for his offense as Chamberlain, but the Celtics center often made an offensive impact regardless of who was defending him.

Opposite left: Chamberlain battles the Celtics' Satch Sanders for a rebound while Russell stands ready to help.

Opposite right: The Russell-Chamberlain rivalry became even hotter when Wilt joined the Los Angeles Lakers which had been frustrated so often in their title games against Boston.

Opposite below: Chamberlain holds the ball that he used to establish an NBA scoring record of 20,884 points in 1966. He finished his career with 31,419.

observed: "If Russell took Wilt to dinner, he must have had an ulterior motive. I always felt he was toying with Wilt, psyching him out. If we were up by 20 points, Russ would lay off and allow him to score 17 points, then come back and shut him off. Afterward, Wilt would look at the boxscore, see that he had outscored and maybe out-rebounded Russell and felt he had won the battle.

"In the meantime, the win went into our column, and Russell cared about that most of all. He also didn't want to give Wilt any extra motivation the next time he played against him. At the end of each season when we had another title and Wilt was home watching, Russ knew he had won."

Chamberlain always pointed to his lifetime statistics compared to those of Russell as proof that he never really lost the battle. In regular season and playoff competition, he accumulated more than 27,000 rebounds, 2,000 more than Russell; and he won the NBA rebounding title in eight of the 10 seasons they opposed each other.

Russell can point out – but he never has – that he still holds the career record for rebounds in the playoffs, when titles are won or lost.

Russell never minded Chamberlain's emphasis on statistics because it was part of his mind game to keep Wilt's

Left: Russell reworked the way basketball was played in the NBA with his defense, but he also had the benefit of playing with a talented Celtics team of unselfish role players.

Below: Russell had the last laugh on Chamberlain and his gaudy offensive statistics as he led the Celtics to 11 NBA championships during his 13 seasons. He had a 3-0 edge over Wilt in head-to-head competition in the NBA Finals.

Opposite above: Larry Bird received the Eastman Award as the nation's top collegiate basketball player in 1979 after leading his Indiana State team to an unbeaten regular season.

Opposite below: Larry vs. Magic for the first time in the 1979 NCAA Finals. Johnson won that tussle with ease.

awesome talents somewhat anaesthetized. In fact, Russell often claimed that he and Wilt were fast friends away from the game and even during the season on days when they played against each other.

"When we were in Philadelphia," recalled K. C. Jones, Russell's best friend and a former teammate, "we would have dinner at Wilt's mother's house and then drive to the game together. Instead of getting himself psyched up to play his foremost rival, Wilt was being the genial host and having a good time. Russell could block all that out of his mind, and when he walked on the court, the good times of a few hours earlier were totally forgotten."

Sam Jones, another teammate of Russell's, recalled the time he had picked up a wooden photographer's stool to defend himself when Wilt chased him around the court during a game in Boston.

"Thankfully, someone broke up the fight," he recalled. "But the next time we were in Philly, Wilt came over to our hotel and took me to his mom's house for dinner. His mother asked me if I really intended to hit her boy with that stool and I said, 'Yes ma'am, I did.'"

Chamberlain was a great competitor whose personal pride was often underestimated because of his reputation of being able to do anything he wanted on the court, but ultimately losing the battles against the Celtics. This always frustrated him.

In the late sixties, Chamberlain even altered his game to concentrate more on defense, like Russell. In the 1968 Eastern Conference playoffs, Wilt and his Philadelphia 76ers zoomed to a 3-1 lead, but the Celtics tied the series, and played the clinching game in Philadelphia. Chamberlain had disdained his scoring binges, content to distribute

the ball to forwards Luke Jackson and Chet Walker, and control the middle as Russell did.

But Russell, then the playing-coach of the Celtics, beat Chamberlain at his own game. He inserted 260-pound center Wayne Embry into the lineup to match strength against Wilt to keep him off the boards, and he went out and played Jackson, a 6'8", 250-pound forward who could not match Russell's quickness or athletic ability. In one fell swoop, two of the 76ers' best weapons were neutralized – Chamberlain took only two shots and scored just two points in the second half, and Jackson was shut down by Russell. Boston won, 100-96, as the Celtics became the first team ever to come from a 3-1 deficit to win a championship.

LARRY BIRD VS. MAGIC JOHNSON

"We weren't about stats. We were about winning." That is how Earvin (Magic) Johnson once summed up the rivalry between himself and Boston Celtics star Larry Bird.

Unlike the Russell-Chamberlain rivalry in which the two players continually banged against each other, the Larry-Magic duels were rarely physical because Bird was a forward and Johnson was a guard, and they never guarded each other. Instead, this was a duel of the greatest players of two great teams . . . Bird and his Celtics vs. Magic and his Lakers.

This was one of the NBA's most special rivalries, born when the two players faced each other for the NCAA championship in 1979. They entered the NBA together a few months later, and for more than a decade their spectacular abilities lit up the court. Both were gone from the NBA after the 1992 season, using as their last hurrah the opportunity to play as teammates on the U.S. Dream Team that won a gold medal in the 1992 Olympic Games.

Throughout the eighties, their skills epitomized the best in NBA basketball. The rivalry existed on the individual and the team level – the Celtics-Lakers rivalry that had played white hot during the sixties was revived; and Bird and Johnson became the focal points of their teams' success, even though both were surrounded by great supporting casts.

Unlike Russell and Chamberlain who faced each other many times each season during six of the 10 years their teams were members of the same conference, Bird and Johnson's teams met only twice a year for the 12 seasons they were in the NBA together; and three times in the

playoffs – a total of 37 games in which Johnson had a 22-15 edge (11-7 in the regular season and 11-8 in the playoffs).

Johnson, for one, appreciated the matchup because it was a measuring stick of his own abilities. "Athletes live to get so up that they can't sleep for two or three days before a competition," he once observed in *Sports Illustrated*. "Nobody did that to me except Larry Bird. The only time in my

life I was ever scared about a game was the NCAA final and those Celtics games. After God and my father, I respected Larry Bird more than anyone."

The rivalry began in the 1979 NCAA championship game between Bird's undefeated Indiana State team and Johnson's Michigan State Spartans. Bird was a senior and Johnson a sophomore. Bird's great all-around ability was largely responsible for bringing his team to the brink of a title.

It wasn't much of a game, though it still attracted the highest TV ratings ever for an NCAA title game. "I thought we'd win because we hadn't lost all year," Bird recalled. "But after about 35 minutes I knew they had the better team. I've never looked back on that game. The best team won."

Bird scored 19 points on a very lukewarm 7-for-21 shooting night while Johnson hit a torrid 8-of-10 and finished with 24 points, also displaying the passing skills that would become his NBA hallmark.

Their first NBA encounter on December 29, 1979, had all the ballyhoo of a motion picture world premier – and why not, since it was played in Los Angeles at the Fabulous Forum and one of the principals was already known simply as Magic.

The Lakers won 123-105 and Johnson won the statistical edge with 23 points, eight rebounds and six assists to Bird's 16-3-3 line. From that point to the last time they faced each other as rivals in 1991, the only comparison would be which team won and which team lost, and who had the better statistics.

"On a personal basis, we had to be content with getting the best of each other at odd times during a game," Johnson said later. "In one game, I was back on a fast break and somebody kicked the ball out to him so I had to run to get

Larry on the wing. Larry says, 'What are you running out here for? You know it's too late.' And he buried it in my face."

Actually, the rivalry didn't heat up until their fourth season in the league because Johnson missed three of the first five encounters with injuries and was badly hobbled in a fourth. Neither team played each other in the playoffs but they never lost track of each other.

"When the new schedule came out each year," Johnson once recalled, "I'd grab it and circle the Boston games. To me it was The Two and the other 80. During the season, I'd check out Larry's line first thing. If he had a triple-double, I knew what I'd want that night. But what would get me would be his big ones, when he had 20 rebounds. I'd say, 'I'd better get me 20 assists tonight.'"

It was no different with Bird. "The first thing I did every morning during the season was look at the box scores to see what Magic did," Bird also recalled. "I didn't care about anything else."

Johnson was a superb athlete who directed the Lakers' high-powered offense with an almost casual air. His instincts were guided by his own internal radar that often sent no-look passes into the tiniest of openings to become field goals by such stellar teammates as Kareem Abdul-Jabbar and James Worthy.

Bird, on the other hand, was a "plodder," not blessed with all of Johnson's great athletic skills. But his great instincts and natural ability compensated for that, helping him make the right play at the right time. Both were fierce competitors who wanted the ball with the game on the line, and usually made something positive happen when they got it.

Bird and Johnson always played regular season games as if there was a title on the line. Bird had just a one-game

Opposite left: Earvin (Magic) Johnson led Michigan State to the NCAA championship as a sophomore.

Opposite right: The Bird-Johnson rivalry really blossomed in the NBA because they came into pro basketball together as the two most visible rookies in the 1980 season, and immediately took over the leadership roles on title-contending teams.

Right: Magic Johnson helped produce an NBA title for the Los Angeles Lakers in his rookie season, and helped them to four more (1982, 1985, 1987, 1988).

Below: Johnson and Bird played against each other more in the playoffs than in the regular season.

Left: Magic Johnson had retired from the NBA for medical reasons before the 1991 season, but he had one last hurrah as a member of the 1992 U.S. Olympic Dream Team, and took home a gold medal.

Opposite above: Bird and Johnson were teammates on the U.S. Olympic Dream Team, a fitting finale to both of their careers (Bird had retired from the Celtics shortly before the Olympics began).

Opposite below: Bird and Johnson enjoyed their rivalry on the court and became fast friends.

scoring edge on Johnson in their last 11 regular season games; and each of them was tops in their respective rebounding and assists specialties all but one time. Bird's last hurrah against Johnson – and the last time the two faced each other – was a 98-95 win in 1991 in which he scored a triple 11-11 points, 11 rebounds and 11 assists.

The rivalry really heated up when there was a title on the line in 1984 and 1985, and again in 1987. Johnson won in 1985 and 1987. One or both was the focal point in every series.

With the series tied 1-1 in 1984, Magic and the Lakers scorched the Celtics 137-104 in Game 3 in Los Angeles, as Johnson got 21 assists. Afterward, Bird called his teammates "sissies," and called for "12 heart transplants."

It worked in Game 4, thanks in part to a stolen Johnson pass and his two missed foul shots that sent the game into overtime. With the score tied at 123, Michael Cooper fell

down guarding Bird, and Johnson came rushing at him. Bird let the ball fly and it became the game-winner.

Bird led the Celtics in Game 5 with 34 points and 17 rebounds (Johnson had 10 points and 13 assists) and a 121-103 victory at Boston Garden, where the temperature reached 97 degrees.

In Los Angeles for Game 6, Bird again was magnificent with 28 points, while Johnson had 21 as the Lakers tied the series.

In game 7 both players were very workmanlike – Bird with 20 points and 12 rebounds; Johnson with 16 points and 15 assists – but Boston won 111-102. Larry walked away with the title and bragging rights.

That was the last time he had the edge because Johnson and the Lakers won the next two times in NBA Finals – in 1985 and 1987. Their 1985 title clash really was Kareem Abdul-Jabbar's series because he helped rally his team

after a humiliating 148-114 loss that was rubbed raw by torrents of taunts from the crowd at Boston Garden. Bird was his usual steady self but Magic ran the show for the Lakers and kept Jabbar going with his playmaking that was punctuated by a final game triple-double of 14 points, 14 assists and 10 rebounds.

The final Larry-Magic confrontation of great consequence occurred in 1987. No one in the league, including Bird, was playing better than Johnson at this point. He was the key performer for the Lakers, who ran off their second straight six-game victory over Boston. He dominated the series in every respect, turning in 167 points, 78 assists and 48 rebounds. (Bird scored 143, had only a 12-rebound edge and had 32 assists.)

The series' biggest play also belonged to Magic – a running hook shot in the final seconds of the fourth game that gave the Lakers a 107-106 victory and a 3-1 lead in the series, instead of a 2-2 tie.

And just to underscore that bit of "magic," Johnson pulled out another victory the following December in Boston Garden when, with two seconds to play, he took an inbounds pass and fired up a 22-foot bank shot that gave the Lakers a 114-113 victory.

Five years later, Bird and Johnson ended their playing careers together as members of the U.S. Olympic team, a sort of dream come true for both of them to be playing on the same team and combining their talents for a common purpose. Johnson, out of the game a year, and Bird, whose body simply could not withstand the pounding any longer, walked away with their long-coveted Olympic gold medal. They were satisfied.

"People who saw our games against each other saw some of the best basketball every played," Johnson said later. "That's why the Olympics meant so much to me. I had always fantasized about us playing together. For it to happen meant more to me than anything else I've ever done."

HOW IT ALL BEGAN

Dr. James Naismith had a problem. During the winter of 1891 the 18 students in the YMCA College in Springfield, Massachusetts, were on the verge of an insurrection over, of all things, boredom with their physical education program.

In the fall, they had enjoyed football, rugby and lacrosse outdoors; and in the spring they looked forward to baseball outdoors. But it was winter in central Massachusetts; the ground was snow-covered and physical activity was basically an indoor pastime.

The school had tried bringing the fall sports indoors, but cleated shoes, flailing sticks and a hard floor that didn't cushion falling bodies had wrought havoc. Then they tried Army close order drill and calisthenics, but that was no fun. Neither was leap frog or drop the handkerchief or any of the other games copied from grammar school playgrounds.

The murmurs of dissent had reached an all-out roar when Dr. Naismith, a Canadian by birth and education, was given 14 days to solve the problem and quell the "rebellion."

So he went back to his own childhood just a quarter century before when in his hometown of Bennies Corners,

Ontario, he and his friends had played a game called duck-on-a-rock, which involved trying to knock a good sized rock off the top of a boulder by throwing smaller rocks at it from some distance.

Enter: Accuracy.

But he believed that accuracy should occur not by force but by arcing the throw.

Enter: An airborne object.

He recalled that rugby players at McGill University in Montreal, where he had studied philosophy, worked out in the winter by tossing a ball into an elevated box in the gym. Aiming a projectile would also make the game more "scientific." But there were no boxes available for Naismith's purposes.

"How about peach baskets?" the janitor asked him.

Enter: The basket in basketball.

At first the peach baskets were placed with bottoms attached, until it was too much trouble to extract the ball each time a shot was made. The bottoms were removed.

The only place in the gym to hang the baskets was on the balcony, which was 10 feet above the floor.

Enter: For all time, the 10-foot-high basket.

Naismith disdained the use of any sticks, therefore he

Left: The first recognized basketball team in 1891 at Springfield College, including Dr. James Naismith (second row, in suit) who invented the game.

Opposite above: A basketball game in the nineteenth century, with the basket's net sewn together at the bottom, necessitating retrieval of the ball after every successful shot.

Opposite: The New York Renaissance team in 1922, the first great organized pro team. From left: Clarence (Fat) Jenkins, Bill Yancey, John Holt, James (Pappy) Ricks, Eyre Saitch, Charles (Tarzan) Cooper and "Wee Willie" Smith. Inset: Owner Robert Douglas.

Left: Nat (Sweetwater) Clifton of the Harlem Globetrotters, one of America's favorite travelling teams. The Trotters played an annual cross-country exhibition series against a team of college all-stars.

Below: Kenny Sailors of the University of Wyoming, who helped to popularize the jump shot.

Opposite: The Boston Celtics signed Chuck Cooper of Duquesne University as the first black player in the NBA in 1949.

wanted a large ball and settled on the soccer ball. Players were not allowed to run with it, nor could they be blocked or tackled.

At first, Naismith was urged to name his new game after himself – Naismithball – but he demurred and said it should be called "basketball" because it used the peach baskets in scoring points. At the same time, Naismith handed down his "13 Rules," nine of which have been the backbone of the game ever since:

(1) The ball may be thrown in any direction with one or both hands.

(2) A player cannot run with the ball.

(3) The ball must be held in the hands.

(4) A foul will be called for shouldering, holding, pushing, tripping or striking an opponent.

(5) A goal is scored when the ball is thrown or batted from the ground into the basket, and if it rests on the edge of the basket, it cannot be moved by an opponent.

(6) A ball going out of bounds must be put in play within five seconds after the thrower gets it from an official.

(7) A specific number of fouls (at first two, later three and then five or six) would disqualify a player.

(8) The referee will make all rules decisions on the court.

(9) Stipulated time for each half and there can be overtime if the teams are tied at the end of regulation play.

Within a year, the game had caught on throughout the East and Midwest as it began to evolve. The dribble was introduced in 1896; five players on the court became regulation in 1897; the two-shot rule for fouling a player in the act of shooting came in 1911; shoes designed for the game of basketball were first sold in 1917; foul shots had to be shot by the player fouled in 1923; the fast break was introduced by coach Frank Keaney of Rhode Island State College in 1930; the jump shot was popularized by Kenny Sailors of

Left: The Original Celtics, one of basketball's early pro dynasties.

Below left: Joe Lapchick (left), a member of the Original Celtics, later became one of the game's great coaches.

Below: Two great NBA stars of the 50s, Bob Pettit (left) and Ed Macauley of the St. Louis Hawks, flank NBA commissioner Maurice Podoloff.

Opposite: Nat Holman, coach of CCNY, whose team won both the NIT and the NCAA tournaments in 1950.

Wyoming in 1933; and Hank Luisetti's running one-hand shot in 1936 revolutionized offense, as did the elimination of the center jump after each basket in 1937.

The first professional league was the original National Basketball League from 1898 to 1903, and it was soon followed by various organizations from all areas of the East. But none had the impact of the American Basketball League, formed in 1926 by George Preston Marshall, who also founded the Redskins of the National Football League. The centerpiece was the New York Celtics, who so dominated the league that Marshall soon ordered them broken up and their players sent to other teams.

But that didn't work either because three of them – Joe Lapchick, Nat Holman and Pete Barry – went to the Cleve-land Rosenblums and that team became so dominant that it killed the league by 1929.

Four years later in 1933, the NBL was revived and played primarily in the East, then in 1937, expanded to more than a dozen Midwestern cities. It lasted until 1949, when it finally merged with the new Basketball Association of America that was formed after World War II by Maurice Podoloff, a Connecticut lawyer and commissioner of the American Hockey League, whose partners were operators of large arenas in 11 Eastern and Midwestern cities (along with Toronto) seeking to supplement a mostly-hockey winter schedule.

That marriage became the National Basketball Association – the NBA.

IT ALL STARTED IN COLLEGE

Many of the NBA's greatest players also produced some of the greatest moments in college basketball history, sometimes matched up against opponents with whom they later would duel several times a season in the NBA. Their college games were key indicators of how they would play as professionals, and almost without fail they repeated those kinds of performances many times over.

Here are some of the most memorable by players who became legends in the NBA.

Below left: UCLA center Lew Alcindor (with ball) goes high for a hook shot against the St. Louis Billikens in 1967. Alcindor became the legendary Kareem Abdul-Jabbar with the Los Angeles Lakers in the 1970s.

1956 NCAA CHAMPIONSHIP GAME

For two complete seasons, from the fall of 1954 until the early spring of 1956, the University of San Francisco's Dons lost only one game. The Dons were led by center Bill Russell and guard K. C. Jones, two players of opposite temperaments, size and physical skills who were thrown together as freshman roommates but who became lifelong friends and celebrated together some of the greatest successes in basketball history.

Russell, abetted by Jones, Mike Farmer, Harold Perry and Carl Boldt, was the Dons' star well on his way to establishing an intimidating style of defensive play.

Jones was, in a number of ways, a smaller version of Russell. He could all but glue himself to the opponent's offensive star for suffocating defense; and on offense,

he was an unselfish director whose passing was crisp and accurate.

In 1955 the Dons had finished their unbelievable season by defeating defending NCAA champion LaSalle 77-63 to win the title. In the title game San Francisco coach Phil Woolpert had put K. C. Jones on LaSalle's great All-America forward Tom Gola, and Jones had limited him to 16 points, eight below his season's average. Russell controlled the middle by grabbing 25 rebounds, and he scored 23 points. No one counted blocked shots in those days but there was a blizzard of them.

In 1956 the Dons had two objectives: to crash the supposedly impenetrable 40-straight-wins barrier, and to win a second straight NCAA title.

Right: Center Bill Russell is carried off the court on the shoulders of University of San Francisco fans after he led his team to the first of two consecutive NCAA titles in 1955.

They defeated Pete Newell's California team and its deliberate slow-down game, 33-24, to hit the 40-win mark; and then kept on going, undefeated, to the finals of the NCAA tournament. Both Dayton and Louisville, the two best teams behind San Francisco, opted to play in the NIT tournament in New York City (schools had that option then, since the NCAA had only a 24-team field).

Though the Dons lost Jones before the tournament because his eligibility expired, Gene Brown, a better outside shooter, stepped in and helped the team get that second NCAA title with an 83-71 victory over Iowa for their 55th straight victory.

There were many skeptics in the pros who said that the defensive-oriented style of both Russell and Jones wouldn't work in the NBA. Russell killed that notion before his rookie season had ended, and when Jones joined the team after an Army stint, he added the same skills to the Celtics' backcourt. Between them they won 20 NBA championships – not bad for a couple of guys who weren't supposed to make it in the NBA.

Left: K.C. Jones, Russell's college roommate, was an integral part of the Dons' two-season championship run. Both became NBA stars with the Boston Celtics.

Opposite: Russell was a great shot blocker in college, as he demonstrates by blocking one by Iowa's Milt Scheurrman during the Dons' 83-71 1956 NCAA championship game victory.

Opposite below: The 1956 University of San Francisco Dons achieved a record-setting 55 straight victories.

1957 NCAA Title Game

Unbeaten seasons suddenly became epidemic. After San Francisco's perfect 1955-56 season, North Carolina's Tar Heels strode onto the national scene for the first time under coach Frank McGuire, and were unbeaten when they faced the Kansas Jayhawks and their 7′1″ center Wilt Chamberlain for the 1957 championship.

Chamberlain, from Philadelphia, had been the nation's most recruited player two years earlier and had chosen Kansas where the venerable Phog Allen, who was forced to retire the year Wilt arrived, had noted: 'We could win the championship with Wilt, two sorority girls and a pair of Phi Beta Kappas.''

In 1957 the Tar Heels were mainly players coach Frank McGuire had recruited from his friendly precincts in Brooklyn, where he had successfully coached St. John's University in the early fifties. Their star was forward Len Rosenbluth who averaged 28 points a game. It was per-

fect chemistry that got them through three overtimes to defeat Michigan State 74-70 in the semifinals of the NCAA tourney.

Chamberlain, who had averaged nearly 30 points a game to go with over 500 rebounds during the Jayhawks' 21-2 season, had helped his team derail San Francisco's hopes for an unprecedented third straight NCAA title by winning 80-56 in the semifinals. There was no denying that North Carolina and Kansas were the two best teams in the country, but everyone gave the edge to Kansas because of Chamberlain.

But Frank McGuire had some city slicker in him. He believed that, when necessary, it was as possible to out-psyche an opponent as it was to outscore him. So he sent out the Tar Heels' shortest starter, 5′11″ guard Tommy Kearns, to take the center jump against Chamberlain.

"I told him if he jumped high enough, he might reach

Left: Wilt Chamberlain (13) and the 1957 Kansas Jayhawks after he led his team to the Big Seven Conference tournament title and a spot in the 24-team NCAA tournament.

Opposite: Chamberlain (with ball) is guarded by North Carolina star Len Rosenbluth in the 1957 NCAA title game, won by the Tar Heels 54-53 in a record-setting three overtimes.

Wilt's stomach," McGuire said later, also explaining it was foolish to "waste" his own center, 6'9" Joe Quigg. "The big thing was that Wilt looked freakish standing there so far above our man, and I knew it would get to him because he still was a kid . . . and kids are kids in how they react to certain situations."

McGuire also put Quigg on the outside to force Chamberlain away from the basket to cover him. McGuire's strategy worked well, rattling Chamberlain so much that it took him five minutes to score his first basket. Len Rosenbluth rose to the occasion and scored 14 points as the Tar Heels, shooting at a torrid 64 percent, led 29-22 at the half.

In the second half, Kansas reestablished its game, and with less than two minutes to play the Jayhawks led 46-43. Rosenbluth fouled out after scoring 20 points but Quigg added a field goal and, following a Kansas turnover, Kearns tied the score with a foul shot just before the end of regulation play.

Rosenbluth's replacement Bob Young and Chamberlain

each scored a field goal in the first overtime; and incredibly, neither team scored in the second five minutes, even with Chamberlain's dominating presence.

In the third overtime North Carolina pulled ahead, but Chamberlain's three-point play and Maurice King's foul tied the score 52-52 with only a minute left to play. With North Carolina playing for the last shot with a half minute remaining, John Parker of Kansas flicked the ball away from Quigg and into the hands of the Jayhawks' Gene Elstun, who was fouled by Kearns. Elstun made one of two shots and Kansas led 53-52 with 25 seconds to play.

With one last try, Kearns tried to drive around Chamberlain but Wilt batted the ball away – right to Quigg, trailing the play, and he was fouled with six seconds remaining.

The previous night, Quigg had dreamt he won the game with a jump shot. Part of the dream came true as he sank his foul shots and then knocked away a long, last-second pass intended for Chamberlain to end the longest NCAA playoff game ever with a 54-53 North Carolina victory.

UCLA-HOUSTON, 1967 AND 1968

Lew Alcindor, later known as Kareem Abdul-Jabbar, and Elvin Hayes staged one of the most electrifying three-game rivalries in the history of college basketball in 1967 and 1968, and then continued their personal duels for 15 more seasons in the NBA.

Alcindor was an integral part of UCLA's amazing run of seven straight NCAA championships, and twice led the Bruins to victories in NCAA semifinal games over Hayes's University of Houston Cougars. In between, 52,693 jammed Houston's Astrodome and watched Hayes lead Houston to victory over Alcindor and UCLA in the most spectacular non-playoff college game ever played in the United States.

This was one of those rivalries that has its birth at tournament time when two spectacular players are matched against each other. Alcindor was a center, Hayes a forward, and while not contesting each other on a one-on-one basis, they were always the centerpiece of their teams.

In their first meeting, in the semifinals of the 1967 NCAA tournament, Alcindor and UCLA triumphed 73-58. Hayes had won the statistical battle, with 25 points and 24 rebounds compared to Alcindor's 20-19 line, and he was

Opposite left: Lew Alcindor (33) of UCLA battles Houston's Elvin Hayes for a rebound in the semifinals of the 1967 NCAA championship game, the first of three momentous head-to-head battles the two fought as collegians.

Opposite right: Alcindor fires one of his patented sky hooks over Hayes in the 1968 NCAA semifinals. Alcindor's Uclans won head-to-head meetings in the tournaments, depriving Hayes of a collegiate championship.

Right: Hayes had his day against Alcindor with 39 points and 15 rebounds in a 1968 regular season victory at Houston's Astrodome before the largest crowd ever to see an indoor game in the U.S.

unimpressed with his foe. "Alcindor's not, you know, all they really put him up to be. He's not aggressive enough on the boards. Defensively, he stands around."

But Lew went home with the NCAA title a day later.

When they met again in the Astrodome the next season, top-ranked UCLA brought in a 47-game winning streak against number two Houston, which hadn't lost since that NCAA semifinal game. Hayes was the number three scorer in the country but Alcindor had missed the two previous games with a scratched cornea and wore an eyepatch when he battled Hayes.

Whether it was the eyepatch or too much Hayes or UCLA having been forced to enter the building through gate 13, no one can say, but the Cougars won a thrilling game 71-69. Alcindor never was a factor. He made just four of 18 shots and was badly outplayed by Hayes. Elvin – The Big E – scored 39 points on a 69 percent shooting night and added 15 rebounds and several key blocked shots.

Still, Alcindor and UCLA had enough of a supporting cast to take the game to the final 28 seconds before Hayes's two foul shots broke a 69-69 tie for the win.

After the game, UCLA's Lucius Allen sounded a prophetic note: "I hope they get into the NCAA (Final Four) and come to LA undefeated. That would be nice."

And that's exactly what happened. In a second straight NCAA Final Four semifinal matchup, the Cougars' 31-0 record and top ranking disappeared in the rubble of a 101-69 UCLA victory. The number two ranked Bruins led by 44 points during the second half and held Hayes to just 10 points and five rebounds. Alcindor, with perfect vision and a desire to avenge his poor showing two months earlier, scored 19 points and took down 18 rebounds.

"That was the greatest exhibition of basketball I've ever seen," Houston coach Guy Lewis said afterward.

Hayes and Alcindor/Jabbar continued their rivalry in the NBA from 1970 through the 1984 season, when Hayes retired. Hayes, who played with the San Diego/Houston Rockets in two tours but spent most of his career with the Washington Bullets, won an NBA title with the Bullets in 1979 before Jabbar got his the following year. Jabbar, often surrounded by better players, won three of the five NBA championship games in which he appeared.

Bill Walton & the UCLA Dynasty – 1973

When Alcindor graduated from UCLA after the 1969 season, opponents hoped for a chance at the glory. But the Bruins' success continued, reaching an apex in the mid-seventies when center Bill Walton was the prime mover in an 88-game winning streak.

Coach John Wooden, the Wizard of Westwood who won 10 NCAA titles, including seven in a row from 1967 to 1973, was the architect of college basketball's greatest dynasty. It started in 1964 with a 30-0 season, and Alcindor's arrival in the mid-sixties touched off the run that ended in Walton's junior year in 1973.

Wooden based his tactical success on a 2-2-1 zone press defense that forced turnovers and got opponents out of their games. It was the same defense he had used coaching at South Bend Central (Indiana) prior to World War II. It also was the key to his perfect 1964 season when he used the 6'5" center Fred Slaughter, and two great guards in Walt Hazzard and Gail Goodrich.

But when he attracted great centers such as Alcindor and Walton, and surrounded them with such other stars as Sidney Wicks, Curtis Rowe, Henry Bibby and Greg Lee, the tactics became much easier. After Alcindor left, Wooden built his team around forwards such as Wicks and Rowe, and center Steve Patterson, and won two more NCAA crowns – beating Jacksonville University and its 7'1" star Artis Gilmore in 1970, and Villanova in 1971.

Walton's arrival in 1972 touched off two more 30-0 seasons and a pair of NCAA titles. He had no peers during his three years at UCLA. His 6'11" frame, capped by a thatch of red hair, looked as if it had been sculpted from a giant sequoia tree. He was incredibly strong and was more physical than Alcindor around the basket, punishing anyone who got in his way. He also had huge hands and a fiery disposition to go with his great basketball instincts.

He is best remembered for those two back-to-back perfect seasons at UCLA. In 1972 the Bruins won all 30 games, including an 81-76 victory over Florida State for the NCAA title. The team was so good that when Florida State opened up a seven-point lead midway through the first half, it was the biggest deficit the Bruins had faced all season.

In 1973 Walton had the greatest individual performance in NCAA title game history by making 21 of his 22 field goal attempts and added two free throws for 44 points, plus 13 rebounds in UCLA's 87-66 win over Memphis State.

Midway through Walton's senior year, in 1974, UCLA's winning streak was finally ended at 88 when Notre Dame beat them 81-80. Walton hit 12 of 14 shots and scored 24 points, but Notre Dame got great performances from John Shumate and Gary Brokaw, who combined for 49 points. Shumate outrebounded Walton 11-9. There were two ironies: UCLA's last loss had come at Notre Dame in 1971; and it was at Notre Dame in 1973 that UCLA would defeat the Irish to break San Francisco's record of 60 consecutive wins.

Walton and UCLA lost twice more in 1974, the second eliminating them from the NCAA tournament. Wooden continued as UCLA's coach until 1975 when he won his 10th national title, retiring immediately after beating Kentucky 92-85.

Asked later which he valued more – his 88-game winning streak or 10 national titles – Wooden made a candid assessment: "I take pride in the 88 straight because it is equivalent to four straight undefeated seasons. But it doesn't rank with ten national championships, seven in a row."

Left: Bill Walton (standing, sixth from left) and the 1973 NCAA championship UCLA Bruins. It was the seventh straight title for the Bruins.

Opposite: Walton was a powerful force under the basket for UCLA. Here he pulls down one of his 13 rebounds against Memphis State in UCLA's NCAA title game victory in 1973. He made 21 of 22 field goal attempts in that game.

JORDAN VS. EWING, 1982 NCAA FINALS

One of the most sought after players in college basketball history was Patrick Ewing, a seven-foot center from Cambridge, Massachusetts, who had sifted through more than 200 offers before finally agreeing to attend Georgetown University in 1981.

A couple of hundred miles to the south, at the University of North Carolina, a quiet 6'8" player from Wilmington, North Carolina, named Michael Jordan also began his collegiate career, but without any of the fanfare accorded Ewing.

Six months later, they became the focal point of one of the most thrilling finishes in the history of the NCAA championship game, and began a rivalry that burned white hot into the nineties when they became two of the NBA's biggest stars.

Ewing was the centerpiece of Georgetown's "chip-on-the-shoulder, us vs. them" style of basketball under coach John Thompson. Though Thompson was careful to bring him along as slowly as possible, it was hard to slow down Ewing's tremendous talent and the Hoyas immediately became a national power.

Jordan, on the other hand, had to blend in with a very talented team that coach Dean Smith had put together – including future NBA stars such as James Worthy and Sam Perkins – geared around his very exacting style of play.

Both Jordan and Ewing were key players in leading their teams to the 1982 NCAA Finals that were played at the SuperDome in New Orleans before more than 61,000 fans. To reach that pinnacle, the Tar Heels had defeated a fine Houston team featuring Akeem Olajuwon, 68-83, while Georgetown made it past Louisville 50-46.

Ewing set the tempo for the title game when he blocked

Left: Michael Jordan of North Carolina vs. Georgetown's Patrick Ewing in the 1982 NCAA title game. Both were freshmen at the time, yet the game's outcome hinged on their talent.

Opposite left: The game winner! Jordan launches a jump shot with 17 seconds to play and the Tar Heels trailing Georgetown by one point in the 1982 NCAA title game.

Opposite right: Jordan vs. Ewing, NBA style: Their rivalry continued for nine seasons in the pros, and Michael came away with three more titles.

North Carolina's first four shots – but watched in dismay as each of them was ruled goaltending, giving North Carolina a quick 8-0 lead.

But the Hoyas were a resilient team and led at the end of the first half 32-31, though Worthy kept the Tar Heels close with 18 points. With six minutes to play in the game he hit two foul tries for a 57-56 lead. The battle continued, then Ewing's short jumper and Sleepy Floyd's jump shot with less than a minute to play gave the Hoyas a 62-61 lead.

To that point in the game, Jordan had been an unspectacular part of North Carolina's offense, but he had the poise of a veteran. With 15 seconds to play, he stood at the left baseline and calmly swooshed a shot for a 63-62 Carolina lead.

It was an amazing shot but he drilled it so cleanly that he said later, "I didn't understand what everyone was so excited about. It was a shot I could make and I did. It took me a while to realize what it all meant."

Georgetown had one last chance but guard Fred Brown, in a moment of panic, threw a pass that went directly to Worthy, who led all scorers with 28 points, and that sealed North Carolina's victory.

Ewing and Jordan later were teammates on the 1984 U.S. Olympic team and again in 1992 on the U.S. team at the Barcelona Olympic Games, winning gold medals both times. It wasn't until the late eighties when Ewing was the star of the New York Knicks and Jordan was not only the star of the Chicago Bulls, but recognized as the best player in the world, that an on-court rivalry resurfaced.

Again, it was Jordan who had the edge as the Bulls eliminated Ewing and the Knicks in the semifinals of the NBA's Eastern Conference playoffs in six games in 1989; blew them out in three games in 1991; and then after falling behind 0-2 in 1993, roared back with four straight wins en route to winning their third straight NBA title.

But it all began on that frenzied night in New Orleans.

SHOT HEARD 'ROUND THE NCAA: LAETTNER'S 1992 GAME-WINNER

Some teams are fated to win. There are times when a team's destiny just seems foresworn.

Duke's Blue Devils in the 1992 NCAA Eastern Regional Finals was one of those teams. And Christian Laettner became the agent of destiny when he launched one of the most amazing shots in the history of the NCAA tournament – a 20-foot jump shot from outside the foul circle with 2.1 seconds to play in an overtime period, and his team trailing by one point.

Some called it a "desperation" shot, but it all seemed part of some mystical plan that kept Duke moving en route to eventually winning its second straight NCAA title.

Few had ever performed as well as Laettner on this late April 1992 afternoon in Philadelphia's Spectrum. He made all 10 of his field goal tries and all 10 of his foul shots. He had seven rebounds, three assists and two steals against a hotshot Kentucky team. The year before, Laettner broke the hearts of the University of Connecticut in the quarter finals by sinking the winning basket with 1.6 seconds to play.

It looked as if Kentucky's grittiness would pay off when Wildcats guard Sean Wood banked a shot over Laettner's outstretched arms for a 103-102 Wildcat lead with less than five seconds to play in the overtime period.

Duke called timeout immediately.

"First of all, we're going to win, okay?" coach Mike Krzyzewski told his team as he began to draw up a final play, one that Duke had used against Wake Forest just a few weeks earlier. On that occasion, Grant Hill heaved a misdirected pass to Laettner that he caught out of bounds.

"I'm not going to step out this time," Laettner told him.

He didn't have to. Hill's 75-foot inbounds pass was perfectly placed right in the middle of the court. Laettner caught the ball near the free throw lane. He turned, thinking there was just one defender near him but he was faced with two.

He didn't panic, but shoulder-faked to the left, dribbled right with a defender near him and then turned to his left and shot the ball.

"I never saw the ball go through the basket," Krzyzewski said later. "But I've seen Christian shoot so much that when I saw the arc, I knew it was in."

Like it was fate.

Left: Christian Laettner attracted opponents' attention constantly because he was Duke's go-to player.

Above: The ultimate trophy – Laettner holds the net from Duke's winning basket in the 1992 East Regional Finals.

Opposite: Another game winner! Laettner launches a 20-footer with less than two seconds to play to give Duke a 102-101 tourney victory over Kentucky.

KAREEM ABDUL-JABBAR

He began his career as Lew Alcindor, a three-time All-America from UCLA who led the Bruins to three consecutive NCAA Championships. As a pro player he helped the Milwaukee Bucks, who had drafted him number one in 1969, to the NBA Championship two years later.

Before he retired after a record-setting 20 years in the NBA – the final 14 with the Los Angeles Lakers – he also led the Los Angeles Lakers to four more titles.

Throughout most of his career, Kareem Abdul-Jabbar lived up to the raves that had begun even while he was a freshman at Power Memorial High School in New York City in the early sixties. Hundreds of colleges vied for his services before he finally settled on UCLA, where his teams posted an 88-2 record and started on a run of seven straight NCAA titles.

Kareem, who was the NBA's Rookie of the Year in 1970, was primarily a scorer during his early seasons with the Bucks because he was their prime offensive weapon. Oscar Robertson added the same important playmaking dimension to the Bucks that Magic Johnson later would bring to the Lakers, and championships resulted in both instances, in Milwaukee in 1971 and then during the eighties in Los Angeles.

Jabbar developed his famed "sky hook" shot that was unstoppable because his great height and arm span allowed

Above right: Kareem Abdul-Jabbar, then known as Lew Alcindor, led UCLA to three straight NCAA titles after being the nation's most sought-after high school recruit in the mid-sixties.

Right: Jabbar breaks Oscar Robertson's record with his 247th point in the NBA All-Star Game series during his 17th All-Star Game appearance. He finished his NBA career as its all-time scorer with 38,387 points.

him to direct the ball downward, unlike everyone else's shots which had to go up first to go down. He won the first of two consecutive NBA scoring titles as a rookie and finished his career with an NBA record 38,387 career points.

Kareem was a prodigious force under the basket. He holds the NBA record of 9,394 defensive rebounds and he blocked over 3,100 shots from the time the league began keeping such stats. He set a season record of 1,111 defensive rebounds in 1976 and had a record 29 against the Detroit Pistons in 1975.

He also logged an incredible 57,446 minutes of playing time (that's 957 hours or the equivalent of playing non-stop for over five and a half days!) in 1,560 games.

There is little doubt that his greatest seasons came with the Lakers – and the greatest of these didn't occur until Magic Johnson joined the team in 1979. He played on Lakers championship teams in 1980, 1985, 1987 and 1988 – the latter two at the tail end of his career when the scoring and rebounding load was distributed to others on the star-studded Lakers.

He played in 237 playoff games, averaging more than 24 points while pulling down 2,481 rebounds and blocking 476 shots, all NBA records.

Opposite: Jabbar at work with his famed, unstoppable "sky hook" shot. He actually shot down toward the basket thanks to his 7' 1" height and great arm span.

Above: Jabbar was a member of five Lakers NBA championship teams, including back-to-back title winners in 1987-88.

Right: Jabbar also led the Milwaukee Bucks, who had originally drafted him in 1969, to a title in 1971. One of his early great rivals at center was Lakers Hall of Fame center Wilt Chamberlain, whom he later succeeded.

ELGIN BAYLOR

Elgin Baylor was the "man with a million moves" – the "master of the head bob" – and one of the most prolific players in the history of the NBA while spending his entire career with the Lakers, both in Minneapolis and Los Angeles.

He is best described as a "scoring machine" because Baylor was the best pure shooter of the sixties when he led the Lakers to the NBA championship Finals eight times during his 12 full seasons.

He averaged 27.4 points per game during his career, third best in NBA history, and three times he averaged more than 30 per season. His best year was 38.3 in 1962.

Baylor was fun to watch, but he was hell to guard. Satch Sanders, the great Celtics defensive forward during the sixties always got the job. One night after Baylor had set an NBA playoff record of 61 points against the Celtics, coach Red Auerbach told Sanders in all seriousness that he had done a good job!

Whenever Baylor got the ball, usually on the left side of the court, his head would begin to bob up and down as he dribbled to get a good shooting position. His body twitched a bit but the built-in radar that guided his shots was almost evident as he targeted the basket.

He was a 6'5" forward with the mentality of a guard. He could snatch a rebound and dribble through a defense with the deftness of a waterbug, cranking up his series of head bobs and body twitches as he neared the basket before finishing off the journey with a dunk.

Though best known for his scoring, he was a fine re-bounder, getting more than 11,400 during his career. His athleticism enabled him to match centers and forwards six and seven inches taller.

Baylor joined the Lakers as a number one draft pick

from Seattle University in 1958 during the team's final two seasons in Minneapolis. He had capped his college career by winning the MVP award in the 1958 NCAA tournament, though his team lost the title game to Kentucky. He then helped the Lakers to one last Western Division title in the Twin Cities in 1959.

The only disappointment in his career was not playing full-time on an NBA champion because his teams lost in seven more NBA Finals. When the Lakers finally won the title in 1972, injuries had sent him to the sidelines for good.

But nothing detoured his way to the Hall of Fame.

Above: Elgin Baylor of the Los Angeles Lakers drives on the Cincinnati Royals' Jerry Lucas. Baylor had no offensive limits on the basketball court.

Left: Baylor begins one of his patented herky-jerky moves to the basket against the St. Louis Hawks' Bob Pettit.

Opposite: The classic late sixties NBA All-Star Game matchup: Baylor against Oscar Robertson in the 1967 game in San Francisco.

BOB COUSY

Bob Cousy did for the NBA what a bright strobe light does for a night club – he gave it some flash and dash in its early seasons with his up-tempo style of playmaking.

The league was barely able to toddle when Cousy joined the Boston Celtics in one of the most fortuitous picks that team ever made.

Cousy was a member of the 1948 Holy Cross NCAA championship team but the Celtics – located just 40 miles away in Boston – bypassed him in the 1950 draft in favor of 6'11" center Charley Share. Instead, Cousy was drafted by the Tri-Cities Blackhawks in the first round, and then traded a short time later to the Chicago Stags.

The Stags franchise folded before the season began and Cousy's name, along with those of two other veterans, was drawn out of a hat. Celtics owner Walter Brown allowed two other owners to pick ahead of him, and Cousy's slip was the only one left. That bit of dumb luck cost Boston $8,500 – the best bargain in NBA history as Cousy went on to become a catalyst for the team's incredible run of titles.

At first, Celtics coach Red Auerbach thought Cousy's up-tempo style of court-long and behind-the-back passes and fancy dribbling was too flashy. But when he saw its effectiveness, he changed his mind and he allowed Cousy to run the team's offense. The decision paid off because his on-court direction helped the Celtics to six titles in seven years.

Cousy was soon nicknamed "Houdini of the Hardwood"

and millions of young players began emulating his style, which had previously been limited to the Harlem Globetrotters and had been considered simply exhibitionism. But when Cousy did it in the course of competitive play, it became legitimate.

When he retired after the 1963 season, he had accumulated 6,955 assists, then the all-time record, and had led the NBA in assists eight seasons in a row, from 1953-60. But long before this he was recognized as one of the NBA's best guards, beginning in 1952 when he had begun a 10-year streak as a member of the All-NBA team. His contribution was such that he was named the NBA's Most Valuable Player when the Celtics won their first title in 1957, though rookies Bill Russell and Tom Heinsohn had become the team's turnaround players.

Cousy's constant attack on the basket drew many fouls, and he made 80 percent of his foul shots during his career. In a 1953 playoff game against Syracuse, he made 30 of 32 foul attempts, still an NBA playoff game record. In 109 playoff games, his 18.5 points per game scoring average exceeded his 18.4 regular season scoring mark. For his career, he scored 16,960 points with a combination of daring court-length drives, whirling one-handed spinners and hook shots, and old fashioned two-handed push shots from outside the foul circle.

But no matter how he did it, the Cooz knew what to do with the ball.

Far left: Bob Cousy and one of his famed give-and-go passes to Celtics teammate Tom Heinsohn. Such tactics made him the ultimate on-the-court creator.

Left: Cousy was a member of the Holy Cross 1948 NCAA title team.

Opposite top: Ball control and dribbling in tight places, as demonstrated here against the Lakers' Jerry West, were a Cousy hallmark.

Opposite: Cousy was a proponent of a "bombs away" offense whenever he had a chance.

Opposite far right: Cousy and Celtics coach Red Auerbach, who had passed him over in the draft but got a second chance in a dispersal of players from the defunct Chicago franchise in 1951.

JULIUS ERVING

Julius Erving taught basketball players how to fly.

While still a star in the old American Basketball Association with the Virginia Squires and New York Nets, he became known as Dr. J, and his "house calls" were a series of swooping, leaping, soaring drives to the basket, some of which seemed to start at midcourt.

Never mind that he may have carried the basketball in contravention to the strict interpretation of the traveling rule, he was colorful and dynamic, and pro basketball fans – certainly the young ones – loved his style.

Though Michael Jordan would popularize this style in the eighties, it was Erving who first got the nation's attention with his flying-through-the-air antics. His style was still somewhat reserved during his three years at the University of Massachusetts, where he was one of just seven players in NCAA history to average 20 points and 20 rebounds a game. But when he got into the free-wheeling ABA, then the sky – literally and figuratively – was the limit.

In his five years with the ABA before it was merged with the NBA and he was traded to the Philadelphia 76ers, he

Left: Julius Erving and his University of Massachusetts coach Jack Leaman.

Opposite top: Erving was a star in both the American Basketball Association where he helped the New Jersey Nets to a pair of titles; and with the Philadelphia 76ers of the NBA, where he won a title in 1984.

Opposite: Dr. J makes one of his famous "house calls" against Kareem Abdul-Jabbar in the 1984 NBA All-Star game.

Opposite far right: Erving was one of the NBA's most exciting offensive players, particularly when he wound up to start a flying journey to the basket.

was the league's greatest star. Erving led his team in scoring three times He was the ABA's Most Valuable Player in 1974 and 1976, and was co-MVP in 1975. He also was MVP of the ABA playoffs in 1974 and 1976 when the Nets won the league title. Erving's 28.7 average was the highest of any player in the ABA's eight-year history.

And the good doctor didn't change an iota when he joined the 76ers in 1976, nor for any of the 11 years when he was one of the NBA's most recognized stars. He was the league's Most Valuable Player in 1981, even though his team was eliminated in the semifinals of the playoffs by the Boston Celtics. He was the catalyst when the 76ers won the title in 1983 in just 13 playoff games; and he was picked to the all-NBA team five times.

During his ABA-NBA career, Dr. J scored 30,026 points, 18,364 of them in the NBA. He had a 23.9 career average, and a 22.0 per game mark in the NBA; and he averaged more than 20 points in his first nine seasons with the 76ers.

Erving's very fine defensive ability often was overlooked. He was a member of the ABA's 1976 all-defensive team and used his athletic ability to accumulate an ABA-NBA career total of 10,525 rebounds. He made 1,508 steals during his NBA career. (The ABA didn't keep steals records but he was one of that league's premier ball hawks during his five seasons.)

But most of all, he seemed to fly through the air with the greatest of ease, often ending his flight with a dunk.

JOHN HAVLICEK

John Havlicek is a tribute to every underrated player who ever worked hard to become a star.

He came to the Boston Celtics in 1962 with a reputation as college basketball's greatest defensive player during his three season at Ohio State – and that's all anyone expected he'd be on a professional level.

Havlicek's work ethic mirrored his efforts on the court. He worked to raise his so-so shooting ability to attain his great offensive skills. In the late sixties, while the Celtics were closing out their great dynasty years, he became a starter because the team needed him on the court as much as possible.

After playing 16 NBA seasons, Havlicek ranks as the NBA's number seven all-time scorer. He played on eight Celtics championship teams, the last four as team captain; 13 NBA All-Star Games; and was an all-NBA selection four times.

Havlicek was a superb athlete – so good that in 1962, he was a first-round choice of the Boston Celtics in the NBA draft and a seventh-round pick by the Cleveland Browns in the NFL draft, even though he had not played football since his high school days in Martins Ferry, Ohio. He gave pro football his first shot as a wide receiver and made it to the final cuts during the exhibition season. "He was just a step too slow," said Paul Brown, the Browns' legendary coach.

He was never too slow on the basketball court, and immediately cut a place for himself in the Celtics' championship era as the important "sixth man," the player who was the first off the bench after the game began with the purpose of maintaining pressure on a tiring opponent with his shooting and defense. That role suited Havlicek perfectly because he was indefatigable. He played in 1,442 playoff and regular season games. He is in the top 10 with his 1,270 regular season games in minutes – 44,471 (or 4.4 days!).

"During a playoff game, I was going as fast as I could and feeling pretty good about it," said Celtics center Dave Cowens, a teammate during the seventies, "when John came running past me and told me to stop lagging. And the guy was almost 10 years older than I was."

When Havlicek retired in 1978, Celtics general manager Red Auerbach, who also coached Havlicek for four years, declared that even at age 38, he left the game at least four years too soon. "He could have played with great excellence past 40, he was that kind of athlete," Auerbach said. As a consolation, during his early retirement years, Havlicek often scrimmaged against the front liners, including Larry Bird; and Bird, 15 years younger, found it difficult to cope with him.

Nicknamed "Hondo," he still maintained his bulldog approach to defense and was named to the NBA's all-defensive team five times. Just as everyone said he would.

Opposite left: John Havlicek forged a reputation as a fine defensive player with Ohio State's NCAA champion team.

Opposite: Havlicek made a reputation as the Celtics' famed "sixth man."

Above: Havlicek, shown driving against the Bucks' Oscar Robertson, developed his offensive skills with the Celtics.

Above right: Havlicek played both guard and forward with the Celtics during his 16-season career.

Right: For someone who came into the NBA with only a reputation for defense, Havlicek had a remarkable turnaround as he finished among the NBA top ten all-time scorers with over 26,000 points.

GEORGE MIKAN

George Mikan was the Shaquille O'Neal of his day. The huge, overpowering, 6′10″, 245-pound center dominated his position for the last half of the forties and the first half of the fifties when pro basketball and specifically, the National Basketball Association, began to grow its roots.

It was a different, slower game back then when teams were more deliberate on the court and players, particularly centers, were not required to be mobile, athletic performers. And Mikan was the NBA's first great star, a player against whom other centers were measured until Bill Russell and Wilt Chamberlain established new standards for the position.

Mikan dominated everyone during his nine full seasons as a pro. While at DePaul, he improved some ordinary physical skills when coach Ray Meyer put him on a rigorous regimen of rope skipping, shadow boxing and even ballet. He made Mikan learn to shoot with both hands and the big guy soon refined a hook shot that was his hallmark – all but unstoppable with his height and great arm span – for the rest of his career.

Mikan led his teams to championships of three different leagues from 1946 to 1954: the Chicago Stags and Minnesota Lakers of the National Basketball League in 1947 and 1948, respectively; the Minnesota Lakers of the Basketball Association of America in 1949; and the Lakers of the National Basketball Association in 1950, and 1952-54.

He made every all-pro team from 1949 until he retired in 1954 (he later returned to play partial season in 1956 with the Lakers); he made four appearances in the NBA All-

Above: George Mikan was an All-America at DePaul in the mid-forties.

Left: Mikan and his Minneapolis Lakers teammates after he had set a Madison Square Garden scoring record with 49 points in 1949.

Opposite top: Mikan worked to develop his on-court agility through a series of exercises, and he became very mobile for a big man at a time when the game was played at a much slower tempo than it is today.

Opposite: Mikan was an imposing obstacle around the basket and proved the ability of a true big man to succeed in the pro game.

Opposite right: Mikan (left) led the Lakers to three different world championships in three leagues during his career.

Star Game, and was MVP in the 1953 game when he played 40 minutes and scored 22 points with 16 rebounds.

Mikan was a two-time All-America at DePaul University and led the nation in scoring his final two years, including a 53-performance in the semifinals of the NIT against Rhode Island – matching their entire point total in a 97-53 victory – en route to leading DePaul to the title.

The true measure of his greatness is evident by his championships, because the NBA didn't keep the meticulous statistics of today. He finished his career with a 22.6 scoring average in a game that was played without the 24-second clock for all but the final two years of his career. Incomplete rebounding statistics gave him 4,167, including a league-leading 1,007 in 1953 – the second NBA player ever to go over the 1,000 mark – and a 14.4 per game average.

Perhaps the truest measure of his greatness was spelled out one night on the marquee at Madison Square Garden in New York City: *GEORGE MIKAN VS. KNICKS*

BOB PETTIT

When Bob Pettit retired in 1965, he was the NBA's all-time scorer with 20,880 points.

But that he was more than just a scorer was illustrated by the fact that when the NBA selected an all-time team for both its 25th and 35th anniversaries, he was selected to both teams – long after the new breed of scoring/rebounding forwards and centers had time to carve their niche in the league's history.

Pettit was the NBA's premier offensive player during the last half of the fifties and early in the sixties. In 1956 he was the NBA's top scorer and rebounder, one of just three players ever to win both in one season.

That led to the first of his two MVP awards. The other came in 1959, when he won his second scoring crown with 2,105 points and a 29.2 average. His team didn't win the NBA title in either of those MVP seasons, making his selection an even more remarkable feat.

Few could cope with the 6'9", 220-pound forward under the basket, and that is why Pettit was among the leaders in foul tries during those seasons (he led the league in 1956, 1957 and 1959). He was a very smooth shooter with a deadly jump shot that was almost impossible to defend because of his height and arm span. He had six games of more than 50 points and held the single game record of 57 in 1961 until it was later broken by the Lakers' Elgin Baylor.

Though he couldn't outmuscle some of the NBA rebounders he knew how to outfinesse them, and finished his career with 12,849 rebounds.

Pettit began his career as a two-time All-America forward at Louisiana State and a number one pick of the Milwaukee Hawks in 1954. Some experts declared that he was too skinny and too light to withstand the pounding of heavyweight NBA duty but he immediately dispelled any doubts in his first year when he scored 1,466 points with a 20.4 average, and was named Rookie of the Year.

The following year, in 1955, the Hawks moved to St. Louis and Pettit won the MVP Award and also was chosen MVP in the NBA's All-Star Game. The latter was the first of three such awards he received in that annual event.

Off the court, he was all class. "As you go along in life and work hard, you reach new plateaus of accomplishment," he once said. "With each plateau you reach, the demands upon you become greater. And your pride increases to meet the demands. You drive yourself harder than before. You can't afford negative thinking so you always believe you'll win. You build an image of yourself that has nothing to do with ego – but it has to be satisfied. When I fall below what I know I can do, my belly growls and growls. Anytime I didn't play to my very best, I could count on a jolt of indigestion."

Left: The St. Louis Hawks' Bob Pettit (9) retired in 1965 after 11 seasons in the NBA as the all-time scorer with 20,880 points. That mark has since been surpassed more than a dozen times, but he has had no peers as a pure scorer.

Opposite: Pettit led his team to the 1958 NBA championship, and in 1959 he was chosen as the NBA's Most Valuable Player. Here he receives the MVP trophy from Murray Olderman of Newspaper Enterprises Association (center), and NBA commissioner Maurice Podoloff.

OSCAR ROBERTSON

Oscar Robertson was preordained to be a great player from the time he stepped onto the court at Crispus Attucks High School in Indianapolis in 1952 – and he never lost the touch to his final seasons with the Milwaukee Bucks in the early seventies.

Robertson, a 6'5", 220-pound guard in the NBA, was one of the few backcourt players who could dominate an opponent. At the University of Cincinnati, he was named College Player of the Year and first team All-America in each of his three varsity seasons; and he became the first player to lead the nation's scorers in each of them as well.

In his final collegiate season, prior to becoming co-captain of the 1960 gold medal U.S. Olympic team in Rome, he averaged 33.7 points per game.

A number one pick of the Cincinnati Royals in 1960, the Big O played 10 seasons in the Queen City, was named the NBA's MVP in 1964, and made the first team all-NBA each year.

He brought a dual threat to a game – much as Magic Johnson did a decade later – because he became a great scorer and the greatest playmaker in the sport, retiring as the all-time assists leader in 1974. Johnson later surpassed him.

He led the NBA in assists six times and finished his career with a 25.7 scoring average. He averaged 30 or more points a game in six of his first seven seasons. Only Wilt Chamberlain and Michael Jordan approached that mark.

Oscar made the game seem almost effortless with his free-flowing style of play. He could drive to the basket with speed and power; he had a good outside shot; and he controlled his team's tempo of play with his direction. Too often, it seemed the Royals looked to him to do it all, and try as he might, it wasn't always possible.

Robertson didn't win an NBA title until he was traded to the Milwaukee Bucks where, in his first season, he teamed with Kareem Abdul-Jabbar. Robertson's great on-court savvy and his ability to consistently get the ball to Jabbar was the perfect combination for that title ride.

Opposite: Oscar Robertson (second from right) and Jerry West (second from left) were co-captains of the 1960 U.S. Olympic team that won a gold medal in the Rome Olympics. Until the 1992 U.S. Dream Team was formed, it was considered the greatest U.S. team of all time.

Right: Robertson (14) – the Big O – was one of the greatest all-around players in NBA history. Though a guard, he battled bigger players, such as the Celtics' Bill Russell (left) and Jim Luscotoff, for rebounds, and is the NBA's fifth all-time scorer.

Below: Robertson, who never won an NBA title during ten seasons with the Cincinnati Royals, got one in his first season with the Milwaukee Bucks after teaming with Kareem Abdul-Jabbar.

Below right: Robertson receives the NBA's 1964 Most Valuable Player award from NEA's Murray Olderman, whose organization sponsored the trophy.

DOLPH SCHAYES

Professional basketball was primarily located in mid-sized cities throughout the East and Midwest when Dolph Schayes joined the National Basketball League in 1948 after four years at New York University. He was the first-round pick of the Tri-Cities Blackhawks, but shortly thereafter he was traded to the Syracuse Nationals.

When the NBL and the Basketball Association of America merged in 1949 to form the National Basketball Association, Syracuse stayed in the league and Schayes became one of the sport's brilliant early players.

For 16 years he was a prolific scorer and rebounder, and also one of the most tireless players in the game's history. He played 1,059 regular season games during his 16-year career, and from February 1952 until December 1961, he played in 765 consecutive games.

Even injury didn't keep him out of action in 1952 when he broke his right, or shooting, wrist. A cast was applied but he continued to play. "The cast made me work on my left-handed shots, which soon improved," he later said. "Later, when I broke my left hand, my right-handed shots also improved."

He was chosen for the All-NBA team six times, and he was the first player ever to officially record more than 1,000 rebounds in a single season when he grabbed 1,080 in 1951 – the first year such statistics were kept – and that record lasted for three seasons. He also hit the 1,000 mark in 1957 and 1958.

Schayes, a 6'8", 220-pound forward, averaged 18 points per game, a lower figure than some stars, because he bridged the two eras of post-war pro basketball. Until 1954 when the 24-second clock was instituted, the game was played at whatever tempo the coaches desired and point totals were modest. Centers were the most important players both before and after this time, but Schayes carved out a niche as a forward (in the days when there was no distinction between power forwards, which he would have

Left: Dolph Schayes was the same fiery competitor when he played for New York University, seen here against St. Louis University in the 1948 NIT, as he was during his 16 pro seasons.

Opposite top: Schayes led the Syracuse Nats to the 1955 NBA championship – the only title the team won while playing in upstate New York.

Opposite: Schayes (4) was the first NBA player ever to officially grab more than 1,000 rebounds in a season when he had 1,080 in 1951, the first season such statistics became official.

Opposite right: Though Schayes played part of his NBA career in the pre-24-second clock years, he still averaged 18 points a game during his career.

been, and small forwards) with his scoring and rebounding.

Schayes was a meticulous player, thorough in every facet of the game. He was one of the NBA's best foul shooters and led the league three times in accuracy and twice in points. He also was one if its hardest workers and was among the leaders in accumulating fouls.

His signature was running downcourt after he had scored a basket, fist clenched above his head. He also was one of the last of the two-hand set-shooters and had made it a deadly art that he complemented with his strong drives to the basket.

His only championship came in 1955 with Syracuse when George King sank a foul shot with 10 seconds to play and the score tied 91-91. For the playoffs Schayes averaged 19 points per game and grabbed 141 rebounds, his best post-season performance ever.

Schayes was elected to the Hall of Fame in 1972. He also had a successful career as coach with the Philadelphia 76ers, where he was NBA Coach of the Year in 1976. He later had the satisfaction of watching his son Dan put together his own distinguished NBA career.

JERRY WEST

Pound for pound, inch for inch, there was never a better guard in the NBA than Jerry West. His diverse achievements included being a prolific scorer, dishing out 6,238 assists during his 14-season career with the Los Angeles Lakers, and perhaps best of all in a sport where scorers get most of the recognition, making the NBA's All-Defensive team four times – and doing so at the tail end of his career when physical skills are expected to diminish.

West was a first-round draft pick of the Minneapolis Lakers – the second player taken in the 1960 NBA draft – and three months later he followed the team to the West Coast before he had even played a game.

A two-time All-America at West Virginia West was nicknamed "the hick from Cabin Creek" – a total misnomer because he was a most erudite person. The 6'2", 185-pound guard was MVP of the 1959 NCAA tournament, though West Virginia lost the title by a point to California after he had scored 160 points in the tourney. He also was co-captain of the 1960 U.S. Olympic team that won a gold medal in Rome and was considered the best U.S. basketball team until the 1992 Dream Team in Barcelona.

West was brilliant from the start in the NBA. He made the All-NBA first team 10 times between 1962 and 1973, and helped the Lakers to the playoff finale eight times. Unfortunately, he also played during the heyday of the Boston Celtics dynasty and won only one NBA title, in 1972.

He was a deadly shooter. He led the NBA in scoring with a 31.2 average in 1970, and amassed 25,192 points and a 27 points per game average during his career. In four seasons, he averaged more than 30 points per game.

West also was a fine playmaker, with more than 6,200 assists, and he led the NBA with nearly 10 per game during the Lakers' 1972 championship season.

West was a great player late in the game and earned the nickname "Mr. Clutch" because he always called for the ball with the game on the line. Never was this more apparent than in the playoffs, where he established an NBA record of 29.1 points per game. He averaged 40.6 points per game in 1965 against Boston; and in six other years, he exceeded more than 30 per game. He was MVP of the 1970 finals even though, as happened in the NCAA tourney, his team lost.

Opposite below: Jerry West (44) feared no one – not even Boston's great center Bill Russell – when he went to the basket on his patented drives.

Right: West, seen here zipping around the New York Knicks' Walt Frazier, scored more than 25,000 points during his NBA career – all with the Lakers.

Below: West was a three-time All-America at the University of West Virginia in the late fifties.

Below right: West teamed with center Wilt Chamberlain for several seasons before the two finally won the long-sought NBA championship for the Los Angeles Lakers in 1972.

NBA MILESTONES

Over the nearly half century since the NBA was formed and basketball became a wintertime staple, more than 30,000 games have been played and there have been hundreds of exciting moments, many existing today only in the memories of the participants and spectators. Some of these moments have survived as being very special, becoming landmarks that give the game depth and forge its tradition.

The night in 1962 that Wilt Chamberlain became the first – and only – player ever to score 100 points in a game, less than 5,000 spectators were in the Hershey (Pennsylvania) Arena for the game between the Philadelphia Warriors and New York Knicks.

But that event became so singular that today tens of thousands claim to have seen it, just as there are at least a hundred thousand people in Boston who claim to have been in Boston Garden on a June night in 1976 when the Celtics and Phoenix Suns played a dramatic triple overtime playoff game.

And within a decade, there will be a hundred thousand in Chicago who will claim to have been in Chicago Stadium in 1993 when the Bulls and Suns staged a similar battle.

Every team has its own share of great moments . . . in Boston, *Havlicek Stole the Ball* became a best-selling record of great Celtics moments from the 1960s dynasty years and its title came from one unforgettable play that preserved a playoff victory over Philadelphia. In New York the memory of Willis Reed running onto the court in the seventh game of the 1970 NBA Finals against the Lakers will be forever cherished by Knicks fans, and the players from that team are forever adored.

Of such stuff are legends – and the NBA's heritage – made.

Left: Willis Reed tries to get a shot past Wilt Chamberlain in Game 1 of the 1970 NBA Finals.

Right: Michael Jordan en route to scoring a record 63 points against Larry Bird and the Boston Celtics at Boston Garden in a double overtime playoff game, April 20, 1986.

THE BAA'S FIRST TITLE GAME, APRIL 22, 1947

Postwar America was a garden of enthusiasm. Millions of servicemen, happily returning to America to live their dreams of a prosperous civilian life, joined tens of millions more in the nation's first booming economy since the Roaring Twenties.

They also sought new entertainment avenues, especially sporting events. Except for pro football, all of the nation's professional sports venues were located in less than two dozen cities east of the Mississippi River and north of the Mason-Dixon line.

Major league baseball night games had increased, but there were few sports events to attend during the cold weather except for some sporadic pro hockey games and National Basketball League matchups. Organized in the early 1940s, the NBL was primarily comprised of mid-sized cities in upper New York State and the Midwest. Its best team was the Chicago Gears featuring center George Mikan.

Onto the scene in 1946 marched the Basketball Association of America, which was located in five eastern cities, five midwestern cities and Toronto. The league had its usual first season growing pains, but it stayed together and staged its first championship series – the Chicago Stags vs. the Philadelphia Warriors.

The Warriors, owned by promoter Eddie Gottlieb, featured the BAA's greatest star – forward Joe Fulks, whose scoring exploits gave basketball a souped-up look from the low-scoring, walk-it-down-the-court game previously in vogue.

Fulks had played two years at Murray State in Kentucky before the war, and was signed by Gottlieb "more on his potential than on his record." Fulks won the scoring title with a then unheard-of total of 1,557 points, and the earned the nickname "Jumpin' Joe" with nine of the league's 12 best scoring efforts that year.

The teams met in a best-of-seven championship series, and the Warriors romped to the title in five games. Some 10,000 fans jammed dingy old Philadelphia Arena – whose official capacity was 8,200 (an estimated 5,000 more were turned away) – for the clinching game.

The Warriors, behind Fulks, led for the first half, but Max Zaslofsky led the Stags back in the second half and they held a lead until the last three minutes. The Warriors' Howie Dallmar, who wasn't supposed to play because he had calluses surgically removed from his feet that morning, came off the bench and rallied his team, feeding Fulks for the go-ahead shot in an 83-80 victory.

That championship series cemented the BAA's existence, and two years later it was strong enough to absorb the NBL and form the National Basketball Association.

Right: In 1946, the Philadelphia Warriors won the first championship of the Basketball Association of America, the forerunner of the NBA. The team was coached by Eddie Gottlieb (center, in dark suit) and featured the league's top scorer, Hall-of-Famer Joe Fulks (top right). Thousands wanting to see the clinching game against Chicago were turned away from the Philadelphia Arena.

THE NBA'S LONGEST DAY, JANUARY 6, 1951

Overtime games are supposed to be the ultimate sports theater. Imagine the effect of an NBA game that took six overtimes to produce a victor.

It happened once, in an era when there was no 24-second shot clock, when ballhandlers and dribblers could control play for minutes on end, and when both teams thought nothing of going an entire five-minute overtime period without taking a shot.

On January 6, 1951, the Rochester Royals played the Indianapolis Olympians for 78 minutes: 48 minutes of regulation play and six five-minute overtime periods during which only 18 points were scored. Indianapolis won 75-73.

The Indianapolis team, comprised primarily of Kentucky's two-time NCAA champions who also formed the United States' 1948 gold medal Olympic team, had led for much of the game before Rochester tied the score 65-65 at the end of regulation play.

The dull winds of caution overcame both teams as only four points were scored by each in the first four overtimes. Neither team scored a single point in the second and fourth overtimes – in fact, they didn't even take a shot in the fourth OT.

The Royals' center Arnie Risen put Rochester ahead by four in the fifth overtime, but Olympians Ralph Beard and Alex Groza tied the score.

In the sixth, Rochester froze the ball for three and a half minutes, then tried to set up a shot. But with four seconds to play, Indianapolis forced Risen into a desperation shot that missed. Paul Walther grabbed the rebound and, seeing Beard streaking down the court unguarded, heaved a court-long pass that became the winning basket with one second to play.

It was an exciting finish to an historic game that also helped bring about the most revolutionary event in NBA history – the establishment of the 24-second clock that forever changed the way the game was played.

WALTER BROWN'S DREAM:
THE FIRST NBA ALL-STAR GAME

In the early 1950s, a sports fan's greatest fantasies-come-true were baseball's mid-season All-Star Game; the pre-season game between the defending NFL champions and the College All-Stars, the best graduate players from the previous year; and the NFL's Pro Bowl that concluded the season by matching its best players from each conference.

In the fertile promotion mind of Boston Celtics owner Walter Brown came the idea that the NBA, having achieved major league status, should stage its own all-star extrava-ganza prior to starting its playoffs. He played host to the first game in 1951, and some 10,000 fans flocked to Boston Garden to watch the East easily beat the West 111-94.

The result wasn't as important as the establishment of a tradition that now has reached epic proportions as one of the NBA's premier showcases. The event now consumes an entire weekend, complete with slam dunk competition, long range shooting contests, alumni games and extensive hands-on displays for tens of thousands of fans.

Opposite: The Rochester Royals won the NBA's 1951 championship but en route to the title, they lost a six-overtime game against the Indianapolis Olympians. There was no 24-second clock so the teams went a couple of overtimes without scoring and one in which they didn't even take a shot. That bit of dullness became the impetus for the establishment of the shot clock.

Right: Bob Cousy (14) was an annual participant in the NBA's All-Star game from its inception in 1951 at Boston Garden. Today, the game caps an entire weekend of hoop celebrations that is geared as much to the fans as to showcasing the game's best players.

It also allows the game's best players to showcase their skills – mostly offensive – and places the emphasis on having fun.

"It has been an evolving institution within pro basketball," noted Hall of Famer Tom Heinsohn who played, coached and announced more than a dozen of the games. "At one time creativity had to mesh with fundamentals. Now it is a bit looser, with more freedom for the players to jump in and out of the game and do what they do best for as long as they are in."

In the history of the event there have been some great individual performances and some truly great games – none better than in the game's third year, 1954, when Bob Cousy of the Celtics helped the East to a 98-93 overtime victory.

It was the first All-Star Game played in New York's Madison Square Garden, then the unquestioned "Mecca of Basketball." Cousy's set shot had given the East a two-point lead with five seconds to play, but George Mikan sent it into overtime by sinking two foul shots at the buzzer.

Cousy then took over the game. He put the East ahead for good with another two-handed set shot en route to scoring eight of his team's 14 points, then had more than 18,000 fans on their feet cheering with a dazzling display of dribbling and ballhandling.

From that point the game was firmly established and the NBA's pantheon of great stars all have had their special moments in this showcase.

Above: One of the most dramatic moments in All-Star competition was the appearance of Magic Johnson in the 1992 game after he had retired from the NBA for medical reasons. He was chosen the game's MVP.

Left: The All-Star Game always brought out the best in the top NBA stars, such as Wilt Chamberlain (13). They seemed to enjoy competing for recognition with each other as much as competing against each other.

Opposite: The East's David Robinson (50) and Hakeem Olajuwon (54) of the West battle each other in the 1994 All-Star Game.

THE CENTURY MARK:
WILT CHAMBERLAIN'S 100-POINT GAME

During his first two and a half seasons in the NBA, Wilt Chamberlain of the Philadelphia Warriors had been a veritable scoring machine, and pundits were beginning to wonder if and when he would become the first player ever to score 100 points in a game.

The answer: March 2, 1962, at the Hershey Arena in Hershey, Pennsylvania, where the Warriors had moved a home game with the New York Knicks.

In the end, this momentous event was played in relative seclusion. Only 4,124 fans were present. (Tens of thousands have since claimed they were there, some even saying they saw the game in New York's Madison Square Garden!) The game was not recorded with television or movie cameras, and was seen by only a handful of Philadelphia and local area sportswriters.

Signs abound that Chamberlain could do it. He was en route to his record-setting 50 points per game average, and had scored more than 60 points in a game 14 times that year, including a high of 73. On the bus to the game from Philadelphia, he won every hand in a two-hour card game, and

Opposite: Wilt Chamberlain (13), highly touted coming into the NBA, lived up to his reputation and became an offensive force unto himself, capable of scoring as many points in a game as he believed possible.

Above: Chamberlain was inducted into the Hall of Fame in 1979, in part because of his play with the Philadelphia Warriors. He is congratulated by Eddie Gottlieb, who founded the Warriors in 1946.

Right: One hundred points! Chamberlain sinks the basket that gave him 100 points – the only player ever to score that many in an NBA game – against the New York Knicks on March 2, 1962 in Hershey, Pennsylvania.

entering the arena, he passed a shooting gallery that had moving ducks and knocked down every one.

He kept it going in the game against the Knicks, who were without regular center Phil Jordan, and had little behind him. Chamberlain scored 23 in the first quarter; had 41 at the half; 69 at the end of the third quarter; and broke his previous high of 78 with 7:51 to play.

From that point, his Warriors teammates worked only to get him the ball for the 100 points and the Knicks were just as determined to stop him. They tried to stall but Warriors coach Frank McGuire sent out subs to foul quickly so his team could get the ball back.

Chamberlain had 89 points with 5:12 to play, and hit number 98 with 79 seconds left.

With a minute to play, he shot and missed. Al Luckenbill got the rebound and fed Chamberlain, but he missed again. Luckenbill again retrieved the rebound, and when Wilt got that feed, he slammed home his 100th point.

But the strangest thing about the feat was that Chamberlain – a notoriously poor foul shooter – wouldn't have done it without a spectacular 28-of-32 foul shooting performance!

There's a postscript to this story.

When Chamberlain scored his 100th point, there were 46 seconds remaining but the crowd rushed onto the floor and wouldn't disperse, so the officials called the game without it ever being officially completed.

But that was Wilt. Anything to be different.

GUTS BALL, KNICKS STYLE: MAY 8, 1970

The New York Knicks team was a charter member of the NBA, going back to 1946 in the Basketball Association of America, but during the first 24 years of their existence they did not win a championship.

When their all-pro center Willis Reed went down with a badly injured right leg midway through Game 5 of the 1970 NBA Finals, it looked as if the drought would continue.

The series was a battle of wannabes because the Lakers, so dominant during their days in Minneapolis, had been turned back six times in the NBA Finals after moving to Los Angeles and were just as hungry as New York. They had great firepower with center Wilt Chamberlain, forward Elgin Baylor and guard Jerry West.

Arrayed against them was a Knicks team that had set New York afire with basketball fever – Willis Reed, Dave DeBusschere, Bill Bradley, Jerry Lucas, Walt Frazier and Earl Monroe. The Knicks were more defense-oriented than L.A. and it paid off after Reed got hurt because they held the Lakers' offense to just 26 shots, winning the fifth game for a 3-2 series lead.

But without Reed patrolling the middle in Game 6, Chamberlain scored 45 points and pulled down 27 rebounds in an easy 135-113 victory.

The seventh game was at Madison Square Garden, and publicly no one expected Reed to play. But 90 minutes before tap-off, he worked out alone in the Garden, trying a variety of soft shots and checking to see if his leg would sup-

Above: Willis Reed of the Knicks, though hobbled with an injured thigh, battles the Lakers' Wilt Chamberlain for a rebound during the seventh game of the 1970 NBA Finals.

Left: The 1970 NBA Finals between the Knicks and Lakers featured a bevy of future Hall-of-Famers, including (from left) Elgin Baylor of the Lakers, Willis Reed and Dave DeBusschere of the Knicks and Wilt Chamberlain of Los Angeles.

Opposite top: With Reed barely able to play because of injury, other Knicks pitched in, such as Nate Bowman (17) seen here blocking a shot by the Lakers' Jerry West.

Opposite: Reed crumples to the floor after injuring his thigh in the fifth game of the 1970 NBA Finals against the Lakers.

port his movements. Watching silently from a nearby entryway was Chamberlain, and when Willis finished, he walked past his rival and mumbled, "Still can't go to my right."

Wilt laughed because everyone in the NBA knew that was Reed's only apparent shortcoming, but when he reached his dressing room, he told his teammates he could play.

The psychological lift was tremendous because now the Knicks knew they at least had a chance against the Lakers. When Reed trotted onto the floor for pre-game introductions, 19,500 people filled the Garden with cheers.

That sent the Knicks even higher, and when Reed hit his first two shots – the only points he scored in the game – they settled down and played one of their best games of the year en route to a 113-99 victory and their first NBA title.

Reed, though hobbled, played 27 minutes and contributed more with his presence than with his skills. He pulled down three rebounds and did a creditable job double-teaming Chamberlain. But Reed's main contribution was providing the spark so that inspiration could fan the flames.

NOW, THIS WAS OVERTIME: JUNE 6, 1976

The NBA Finals in 1976 featured an improbable matchup: the run-and-gun, hit-the-boards Boston Celtics vs. the come-from-oblivion Phoenix Suns, a team that had been last in February, but in early June had split the first four games of the Finals with the favored Celtics.

The Celtics firmly controlled the series' most crucial game and had a nine-point lead with less than four minutes to play, but they didn't reckon on Paul Westphal.

Westphal, a former number one Celtics draft pick who had helped Boston win the 1974 NBA title, scored nine points in an 11-point Suns burst to tie the score at 94-94 with 39 seconds to play. Curtis Perry's foul shot gave Phoenix a one-point lead. But Boston's John Havlicek tied the game, and had his field goal dropped with three seconds to play, it would have been just another exciting finish.

Instead, it moved to the realm of incredible.

With 1:58 to play in the first overtime, Boston led by four points but Perry scored four straight points to force a second overtime.

With 19 seconds to play in that period, the Celtics led 109-106 until Dick Van Arsdale scored his only field goal and Westphal stole the ensuing in-bounds pass and fed Perry for another score. Phoenix had a 110-109 lead with five seconds to play.

Then Havlicek, the Celtics hero of so many fabulous finishes, banked in a field goal for a one-point lead. The clock said there was one second to play but the Celtics players, believing the game was over, were whooping toward their dressing room.

Above: Paul Westphal of Phoenix battles the Celtics' Charley Scott in the fifth game of the 1976 NBA Finals. Scott and Westphal were traded for each other the previous season.

Left: Referee Richie Powers had a tough night in the Celtics-Suns triple overtime 1976 playoff game. Here, he gets a tongue-lashing from the Celtics' Dave Cowens, and he later was assaulted by unruly fans after the second overtime.

Opposite: (From left) Celtics GM Red Auerbach, coach Tom Heinsohn and captain John Havlicek receive the team's 13th NBA championship trophy from commissioner Larry O'Brien after beating the Suns in six games in the 1976 NBA Finals.

In the middle of the court stood referee Richie Powers, signalling there were two seconds to play. Suddenly all hell broke loose as some fans rushed the court and assaulted him. It took police 10 minutes to restore order to play those last two seconds.

The Suns called an illegal timeout and Jo-Jo White sank a technical foul, giving Boston a two-point lead. But the Suns' Garfield Heard cooly sank a field goal at the buzzer to force a third overtime.

At this point, Celtics coach Tom Heinsohn, suffering from a cold, required medical attention for dehydration. Assistant coach John Killelea took control, and general manager Red Auerbach hustled from the stands to help.

Gone on fouls were Boston's two best rebounders, Dave Cowens and Paul Silas, and in their place came two improbable heros – Jim Ard and Glen McDonald. They scored six points for a 126-120 lead with 36 seconds to play but still the Suns wouldn't die.

Westphal sandwiched a field goal and two foul shots around two fouls by Ard and Boston led by only two points with 12 seconds to play.

But that was it. Both teams had drained themselves and the score stood at 128-126, while the Celtics' Jo-Jo White was able to dribble away the final 12 seconds of the third overtime period. There simply wasn't enough energy left to produce one more miracle.

DR. J GETS HIS RING: MAY 31, 1983

Most of the game's greatest players wear the ultimate badge of honor: a world championship ring. But any who don't – and this is true in any sport – would gladly trade all of the adulation and honors, and even some of the riches they earned, to get that unsurpassable symbol of true recognition and excellence.

In 1983, when Julius Erving's career was beginning to wind down, he had begun to wonder whether he would ever wear a ring with an NBA logo. He had won two championship rings while playing for the New Jersey Nets of the old American Basketball Association, and though they were treasured, they did not grant the same distinction of an NBA ring.

Erving's popularity had soared since he joined the NBA's Philadelphia 76ers. He was the game's most astounding player with his array of swoops to the basket. Dr. J soared over, around and through opposing players in his unique combination of trapeze and ballet.

Yet, he also was frustrated. Since arriving in Philadelphia in 1976, his 76ers had lost three NBA Finals, two semifinals and a second-round playoff series.

In 1983 he was back for a seventh try, this time against

the Los Angeles Lakers, a team which had twice beaten the 76ers in the Finals.

This contest, though, would be different. In 1983 the 76ers had acquired center Moses Malone, a dominant force on the court and the perfect complement to Erving's acrobatic style. They had helped Philadelphia dominate the Eastern Conference, and before the playoffs began Malone guaranteed that his team – and Erving – would win the title when he issued his famous "Fo-Fo-Fo" promise of a sweep.

It seemed to be no idle boast as Philly blew through the first two rounds and faced Los Angeles for the title for the third time in four years. Malone was the perfect weapon against the Laker's Kareem Abdul-Jabbar as he and Erving brought Philadelphia from behind to win the first three games.

In the fourth game the 76ers trailed until late in the fourth quarter before Erving finally put Philadelphia ahead 109-107 with less than a minute to play. Jabbar's foul shot closed the lead to a point with 42 seconds left.

It was time for one final visit from Dr. J, but with a strange twist for him. Though his acrobatics were at their best in this series, he went the conventional route and calmly canned a clinching 18-foot jump shot that soared so majestically it seemed like his personal swan song.

"That shot found me and I just let it fly," he said after his team's 115-108 victory.

And with it, he also found his NBA championship ring.

Opposite: It's showtime for the 76ers' Julius Erving against Kareem Abdul-Jabbar of the Lakers in the 1983 NBA Finals.

Above: Julius Erving wanted nothing more than an NBA championship ring – he already had two from his time in the ABA – to cap his career, and dedicated himself to winning one in the 1983 NBA Finals.

Right: 76ers coach Billy Cunningham (center) puffs on his victory cigar but the smile on the face of Julius Erving says it all, after the 76ers won the 1983 NBA title. Tourney MVP Moses Malone of the 76ers is at left.

MICHAEL THE MAGNIFICENT, APRIL 20, 1986

For most of the NBA's first half century, the Boston Celtics were the league's dominant team. They took great pride – Celtics Pride – in all they accomplished, and considered their famed parquet home court as hallowed ground.

But there were also some blasphemous times on that court – such as the night in 1962 when opponent Elgin Baylor scored a record 61 points in a playoff game, and on a Sunday afternoon in 1986 when Michael Jordan broke that record with 63 points in a double overtime playoff game.

Jordan was the Baylor of his day – a great offensive player who could dominate defenses with a variety of moves and an even greater variety of shots.

In 1986 Michael had missed 64 games with a broken foot and defied Chicago team officials and doctors who wanted him to sit out the entire season by insisting that he play the last 15 games. He then helped the Bulls get the final playoff berth in the Eastern Conference.

Chicago started with a best-of-five series against the Celtics, whose championship team of the eighties was beginning to wind down. Jordan scored 49 points in the first game but Chicago lost.

Three days later and back on the Boston Garden floor, he scored 36 points in the first three quarters with an ease that belonged only to him. "Michael was doing so much and so well that I found myself just wanting to stop and watch him . . . and I was playing," guard John Paxson said later.

At one point in the third quarter, after he arched a soft 20-foot jumper over Kevin McHale, Jordan started repeating to himself as he ran down the court, "All day, baby, allll day!"

In the fourth quarter, Jordan scored 18 of his team's 25 points and hit the 50-point mark. The last two came with no time on the clock – two foul shots that forced the overtime.

Jordan hit a three-point shot with 99 seconds to play in the first overtime to put Chicago ahead 125-121, but the Celtics fought back and forced a second extra period.

Jordan had 59 points by that time and midway through the period, he tied Baylor's record. A bit later, with Boston ahead by two, he flashed past seven-foot center Robert Parish and jammed home his 22nd field goal – and his 63rd point to tie the game for the 13th time.

"Jordan," Parish said later, "does anything he wants on a basketball court, and it's not like he does it in a summer league, either."

That was all for the day because the Celtics scored the last four points and, incredibly, won the game 135-131 – just as they had beaten Baylor's Lakers team on his record-setting night.

But it was left for Bird to put Jordan's performance into perspective: "I didn't think anyone was capable of doing what Michael has done to us . . . I think it's just God disguised as Michael Jordan."

Amen.

Opposite far left: Michael Jordan is congratulated by Bulls teammate Orlando Woolridge after his two foul shots sent the Bulls-Celtics 1986 playoff game into overtime. Jordan set a playoff record with 63 points in that game.

Opposite: Jordan makes one of his 22 field goals over three Celtics defenders.

Above: Jordan was more than an offensive dynamo. Here he leaps high enough to block a shot by 6' 10" Kevin McHale.

Right: Jordan's 63 points broke the previous record held by the Lakers' Elgin Baylor, also set against the Celtics.

FIVE MILLION POINTS . . .
& COUNTING: JANUARY 25, 1988

How far has the NBA come since 1946?

More than five million points, contributed over nearly a half century by a couple of thousand players.

Michael Jordan threw in almost 24,000, Kareem Abdul-Jabbar contributed the most – 38,387, Wilt Chamberlain added 31,419, five members of the Boston Celtics' great dynasty of the sixties – Bob Cousy, Bill Russell, Tom Heinsohn, Sam Jones and Bill Sharman – passed the hat and came up with more than 70,000, and the Celtics' Big Three of the 1980s – Larry Bird, Kevin McHale and Robert Parish – contributed more than 63,000.

So 10,000 here, 15,000 there – and pretty soon you're talking serious points. The NBA never paid much attention to million-point milestones until it came time to celebrate its five millionth point in 1988. The story is intriguing in how the NBA closely tracked the scoring during the season that began with 4,906,649 already in the bank.

Careful totals were kept after each night's games until, when the games of January 24, 1988 were concluded, the leagues was only 450 points short of five million. There were six teams in action the next night – Philadelphia at Washington; Cleveland at Utah; and Milwaukee at Golden state. Given the time zone difference, the games at Utah and Golden State were circled to produce the magic point.

When the 76ers defeated the Bullets 118-117 in overtime, only 215 points were needed. Elaborate communications were set up between the two western arenas and the NBA office where a score-by-score tabulation was kept. Utah and Cleveland were one quarter ahead of the Milwaukee-Golden State game, and the former combined for 103 during the first half. It then became nip and tuck.

At Golden State there was a timeout, while in Utah's Salt Palace, Cleveland's Mark Price was making two free throws with just two seconds to play in the third quarter. 4,999,998.

None of the players on the four teams was aware of this countdown so after Price made his foul shot, Mark Iavaroni of Utah just wanted to get the ball downcourt to teammate Ricky Green, hoping for a successful desperation shot. If it didn't go, then the record would be set in Oakland because that game would resume while the quarter break was in progress in Salt Lake City.

Green grabbed the pass with his back to the basket, turned and heaved up a 20-footer with one second to play – and the ball went in! The near-sellout crowd went wild, completely unaware that the NBA had just recorded its five millionth point.

It took a couple of minutes to make it official.

"Was that last shot good?" one of the people in the NBA office asked Utah PR director Bill Kreifeldt, who was feeding them the shot-by-shot detail.

"Yes, it was," he replied.

"Then you got it, you got the five millionth point!" Terry Lyons, the NBA's assistant director of public relations, cried over the phone.

Just like that.

Opposite far left: Guard Mark Price of the Cleveland Cavaliers did his share to hit the five million point mark against Utah — he hit two free throws to bring the number to 4,999,998.

Opposite: Ricky Green of the Utah Jazz, whose desperation heave in 1988 to beat the buzzer dropped into the basket and became the NBA's five millionth point.

Above: Jazz coach Frank Layden congratulates Green and hands him the ball that recorded the milestone point.

Right: Utah teammate Karl Malone, ''The Mailman,'' delivers a congratulatory hug to Green after his epic basket.

THE DYNASTIES

The most difficult feat in professional sports is to win championships year after year. So much goes into a team winning a title — few injuries, consistently good individual performances, players making key plays at the right time, opponents making mistakes at the right time, and many more ingredients — that it is almost impossible to recreate the same situation from one season to the next.

The first quality for any dynasty is having great direction and leadership. The direction must come from a coaching staff that has as its first commandment: "Do only what makes sense and cut out all margin for error." Then it must insist on — and receive — complete concentration on and compliance with its blueprint for success.

It must also have great players; the more a team has, the longer its dynasty may last. There have been scores of teams during the history of the NBA that have been very talented. But year after year they failed to win a championship because they lacked a key player or two and missed a team chemistry.

That's what happened to the Cincinnati Royals and the Los Angeles Lakers which, during the sixties had such great players as Oscar Robertson, Jack Twyman, Jerry Lucas, Wayne Embry, Jerry West, Elgin Baylor and Rudy LaRussa, but could not match Boston's center Bill Russell and the magical cast of great Celtics players that began a run of winning 11 world titles in 13 years.

It became even more difficult to dominate in the three decades since the Celtics ruled the NBA because the league expanded and talent was more thinly dispersed. Now dynasties are measured in much more modest terms — three titles in a row is an amazing feat; four or five titles over the span of a decade is exemplary.

But creating and maintaining a winner, then turning it into a dynasty team still is the aim of every club — and the hope of every fan.

Right: Michael Jordan captained the NBA's most recent dynasty team, the Chicago Bulls, to three consecutive championships, from 1991 to 1993.

Below: Bob Cousy (14) was the cornerstone of the Boston Celtics' first dynasty, which outlasted his retirement in 1963.

THE MINNEAPOLIS LAKERS, 1948-54

The Lakers were professional basketball's first great dynasty, starting with the 1948 season in the National Basketball League, and finishing with their fifth title while members of the National Basketball Association in 1954.

The Lakers were born as the Detroit Gems of the National Basketball League, but the Gems were moved to the Twin Cities for the 1948 season.

At the same time, the NBL champion Chicago Gears, including center George Mikan, jumped to the Basketball League of America in 1948. That league lasted two and a half weeks but the Gears were denied readmission to the NBL. Their players were placed in a dispersal draft that was based on the inverse order of finish from the 1947 season.

The Detroit Gems had the worst record, and their successors, the Lakers, got the first pick. Welcome George Mikan – and the Lakers' dynasty.

It wasn't all Mikan. Jim Pollard was already with the team. He had gotten the nickname "Kangaroo Kid" during his All-America days at Stanford, where he helped the Cardinals win the 1942 NCAA title, because he was one of the few players in the country who could dunk a basketball. In 1950, after the Lakers' dynasty had begun, they signed Vern Mikkelsen from Hamline University, giving them the NBA's first great front line of Mikan-Pollard-Mikkelsen.

Mikkelsen, the sport's first "power forward," primarily crashed the boards on offense and defense, set picks for Pollard and Mikan, and put back their missed shots.

In the backcourt for most of those seasons were Tony Jaros, who also could play forward, Whitey Skoog and Slater Martin. Skoog and Martin were slick ballhandlers and gave the Lakers' attack its speed.

Johnny Kundla was the team's coach during its dynasty years. Like so many of the Lakers, he had honed his basketball skills in Minnesota and didn't believe in frills or fancy play. He allowed Mikan to dominate the game, and integrated the rest of the players in a well-coordinated attack.

Pollard and Mikan led the team to the NBL title in 1948, beating Rochester. Actually, they won three "world championships" that season, defeating the famed Harlem Globetrotters in a special "world championship" game, and interrupting their NBL playoffs to defeat the New York Rens in the World Professional Tournament in Chicago.

The Lakers, along with Rochester and Fort Wayne, jumped from the NBL to the Basketball Association of America in 1949. Though finishing second, the Lakers beat division winner Rochester, and then the Washington Capitols for the BAA title. Mikan scored 2,002 points that year, including 1,698 during the regular season.

The BAA and the NBL were merged to form the NBA and the Lakers made it three titles in three leagues in three years, winning the NBA's first championship in 1950. Mikan was the undisputed star and scored 40 points seven times that season. The Lakers finished second but beat Rochester in a one-game division playoff, then defeated the Syracuse Nationals in six games for the title.

After losing in the first round of the 1951 playoffs, the Mikan-Pollard-Mikkelsen line produced three straight NBA championships in the 1952-1954 glory years.

The dynasty ended after the Lakers' 1954 title, even though they added two fine players, Dick Schnittker and Clyde Lovellete, the latter tabbed as Mikan's eventual successor. In 1954 they helped beat Syracuse in the Game 7 final, with Pollard scoring 17 points in the 87-80 clinching victory.

Mikan retired after the season, marking the end of a great era for the Lakers, who would later leave the Twin Cities for Los Angeles, to continue their great success.

Right: The heart of the Minneapolis Lakers' NBA dynasty that won five titles from 1948 to 1954. From left: Frank Saul, Vern Mikkelsen, George Mikan, Jim Pollard and Slater Martin. Mikan, Pollard and Mikkelsen formed the NBA's first great frontcourt. Coached by Johnny Kundla, the team also won two other "world" championships in 1948 – against the Harlem Globetrotters and then against the New York Rens in the World Professional tournament.

THE BOSTON CELTICS, 1957-69

Some call the 1957-69 Celtics the greatest sports dynasty of all time – 11 world championships in 13 seasons, including eight in a row from 1959 to 1966. No professional sports team ever had such a championship streak, and none ever dominated a league so thoroughly. The key to this dominance was the play of center Bill Russell.

Red Auerbach came to Boston as head coach in 1950 and soon had a fine array of players, including guards Bob Cousy and Bill Sharman, who later became key parts of the Celtics' dynasty. But they kept missing the NBA finals because they lacked a dominating center.

Then Auerbach worked a trade to draft Russell, and before the center's rookie 1957 season had ended with the Celtics' first NBA title, his great rebounding and shot-blocking had changed the way pro basketball was played.

Soon no one dared challenge the middle with Russell on guard, and he was quick enough to stalk the perimeters and force offenses to work further out. When he rejected shots or grabbed rebounds he kept the ball in play – even able to finish off plays he had started because of his great court speed. A natural leader, Russell would take on the coaching job when Auerbach retired after the 1966 season, winning two titles in three years while continuing to play full-time at center.

Auerbach also blended superb team and role players. Rather than seek a great scorer, he believed that everyone must contribute to the best of his ability. That is one reason why the Celtics had such success against teams with such great offensive stars as Wilt Chamberlain, Oscar Robertson and Bob Pettit.

A second part of Auerbach's winning equation was defense. He believed that it would trigger offense so he demanded that players work hard; and as a third part of his system, pay attention to their own roles. This was best underscored with his "sixth man," a concept enacted first by Frank Ramsay, then John Havlicek. Either could have started but Auerbach wanted someone coming off the bench at a time when the opposition – and even his own team – was starting to tire, and to keep the pace going full bore.

Cousy, a master ballhandler, ran the offense until he retired after the 1963 season; K. C. Jones did it until he retired in 1967; then John Havlicek stepped in, giving up his famed "sixth man" role because he became too valuable to keep on the bench.

Tom Heinsohn, another rookie in 1957, and Sam Jones added scoring. Jones played till 1969, but when Heinsohn retired in 1965, Havlicek and, for the final three years, Bailey Howell were the offensive threats.

Tom (Satch) Sanders came in 1960 and took on the opposition's big scorer in every game. Such role players were asked to go all out for as long as they were in the game – and they included Jim Loscutoff, Don Nelson, Larry Siegfried and Gene Conley.

During the Celtics' 13 dynasty years, their only title game losses were to the St. Louis Hawks in 1958 when Russell went down with an ankle injury during the finals; and in 1967 when they were bested by the Philadelphia 76ers. They won 708 games in that time, with three 60-win seasons.

Opposite below: The Celtics dynasty was keyed by such players as Tom Heinsohn (15, far left picture) and Satch Sanders (16, near left picture). Note the numerous world championship banners hanging from the rafters in Boston Garden.

Right: The conductor for most of Boston's dynasty was coach Red Auerbach, whose victory cigar became his trademark. One of its great constants was center Bill Russell (right), who played on each of its 11 title teams.

Below: The Celtics dynasty began with the 1957 team that included, front row, from left: Lou Tsioropoulos, Andy Phillip, Frank Ramsey, coach Red Auerbach, Bob Cousy, Bill Sharman, Jim Loscutoff. Standing, from left: President Walter Brown, Dick Hemric, Jack Nichols, Bill Russell, Arnie Risen, Tom Heinsohn, Harvey Cohn and vice president Lou Pieri.

THE LOS ANGELES LAKERS, 1980-88

Strictly speaking, the Los Angeles Lakers dynasty lasted from 1980 to 1988, during which time they won five NBA titles and became the first team since the 1968-69 Celtics to win back-to-back championships. They did that by defeating Boston in 1987 and the Detroit Pistons in 1988.

But consider also that from 1959 to 1973 – 15 seasons – they also were good enough to play in 11 NBA championship finals, and won only in 1972. No other team in NBA history saw so much excellence go unrewarded for so long, which is why their success of the 1980s was so sweet.

Kareem Abdul-Jabbar was in his sixth season in 1980 when he helped procure the title that had long been anticipated since his acquisition in 1975 from Milwaukee, and began a run of five titles in nine seasons.

Under general manager Bill Sharman, and later Jerry West, the team restocked its talent larder during the eighties with such offensive stars as James Worthy and Byron Scott; took a page from the Celtics' book and found a great defensive power forward in Michael Cooper; linked them all with Abdul-Jabbar; allowed Earvin (Magic) Johnson to mature as a person and player to run the show; and hired former Laker Pat Riley from their broadcast team to bring it all together as coach.

Riley was a demanding coach, who ignored the distractions of becoming "Hollywood's Team" and brought a strong work ethic to the once-disparate Lakers.

The catalyst was Magic Johnson, who was the team's number one pick in the 1979 draft. The impact was immediate because he used his budding playmaking skills and his enthusiasm to ignite the moody Jabbar and once again made him a great force. As a rookie, Johnson did a remarkable job in the clinching game of the 1980 Finals

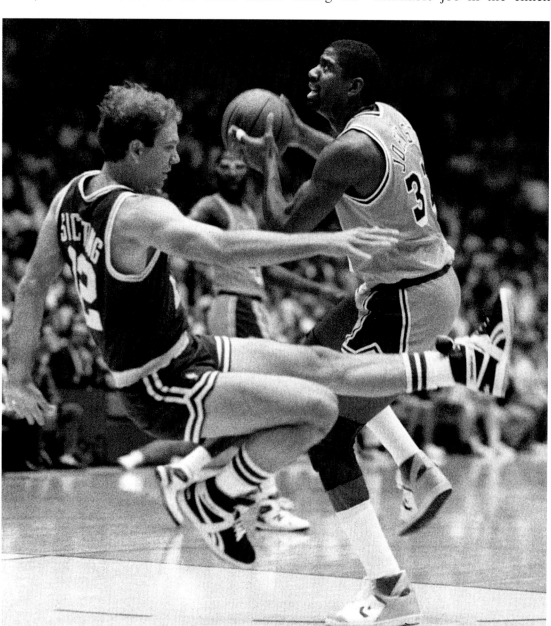

Left: The Lakers didn't become consistent champions until Earvin "Magic" Johnson arrived in 1980. He directed their offense with great flair, and added the sparkle and fire the Lakers needed to become championship contenders.

Opposite top: Kareem Abdul-Jabbar came to the Lakers in 1976 with the belief that he would bring a string of titles to the Lakers, but it didn't happen until Magic Johnson arrived and gave him backcourt help.

Opposite: The Lakers defeated the Philadelphia 76ers twice within three seasons, in 1980 and 1982, to launch their dynasty in the 1980s that produced five NBA championships. Kareem Abdul-Jabbar holds the 1982 trophy in this post-victory photo.

against Philadelphia when Abdul-Jabbar was out with an ankle injury. He started at center and then blended into the Lakers' team approach to key the victory.

The red-hot rivalry with the Celtics for NBA dominance that had flared in the sixties resumed in the eighties. The Lakers defeated Boston for the NBA title in six games in 1985 and 1987; while Boston won in 1984. The on-court rivalry between Boston's Larry Bird and the Laker's Magic Johnson provided continuing story lines throughout the decade, but both teams were so evenly matched that no outcome could be foreseen.

For example, Boston crushed Los Angeles 148-114 in the opening game of the 1985 series, and the Lakers were immediately declared dead. But they ended up winning the title in Boston Garden, the first time the Celtics had ever lost the title on their own court. In 1987 Boston seemingly had forged a 2-2 series tie before Johnson popped in a "baby skyhook" in the final second for a one-point win and a 3-1 lead. The Lakers won the title two games later.

The crowning jewel of this title run for the Lakers was becoming the first team since the 1968-69 Celtics to win back-to-back NBA titles, with a seven-game victory over the Detroit Pistons in 1988. Riley had goaded them moments after they had defeated Boston the previous year when he guaranteed they'd make it two in a row. It wasn't easy. Trailing 3-2, the Lakers fought ferociously for the one-point victory that tied the series. They then rode 36 points and 16 rebounds by James Worthy, then the team's acknowledged offensive star, to a 108-105 seventh game win. It was a glorious end to the Lakers' dynasty era.

THE BOSTON CELTICS, 1981-87

The Celtics seemed on the way back, after slipping from their great dynasty years of the 1960s, when they won NBA titles in 1974 and 1976. But ownership problems sapped their rebuilding energy and Boston soon faded after its 1976 title.

Red Auerbach, the architect of Boston's first great dynasty, almost left the Celtics because of those problems. (He said he changed his mind while on the way to the airport to join the New York Knicks when a cabbie begged him to stay.) He still had some magic left.

In 1978 he drafted Larry Bird a year before his collegiate eligibility expired; and in 1980, he worked trades to acquire center Robert Parish from Golden State and rookie Kevin McHale in the draft, putting in place the NBA's best frontcourt of the eighties and helping the Celtics to five more NBA Finals. They won three of them.

Two coaches led the team. Bill Fitch came in 1979 and he was the right man for starting the revival. Fitch never stopped working and neither did his young team; their efforts accelerated the team's growth after the 1980 season. The revival was abetted by another cast of on-court role players, including Cedric Maxwell, M. L. Carr, Tiny Archibald, Rick Robey and Gerald Henderson, and two years after winning just 29 games in 1979, the Celtics won their 14th NBA title in 1981. Their greatest feat was coming from a 3-1 deficit against Philadelphia in the Eastern Conference finals to go on and beat Houston for the title.

Above and left: Larry Bird became the catalyst for the Boston Celtics' second dynasty run, in the 1980s, with his great all-around play. Bird epitomized the Celtics Pride that helped to produce NBA titles in 1981, 1984 and 1986.

Opposite top: Center Robert Parish teamed with Bird and Kevin McHale to give the Celtics the best frontcourt in the NBA during the eighties.

Opposite: The second generation Celtics dynasty was put together by GM Red Auerbach (with ball) and directed by coach K.C. Jones (fourth from right). This is the 1986 team photo.

Fitch's intensity and his obsessive work demands on his team, combined with his overall insecurity working in the formidable shadow of Auerbach, took its toll and he left after the 1983 season.

Auerbach, seeking to reinvigorate "Celtics Pride" that was born during his own coaching days and had always energized the franchise, named ex-Celtic K. C. Jones as head coach. K. C. had led the Bullets to the NBA Finals in 1979.

The Bird-Parish-McHale troika was superb. Bird was the acknowledged star – a hard-working player who was not only a marvelous offensive player but unselfishly dished out hundreds of assists each year, was tough on defense and dove on the floor after loose balls in the best tradition of Celtics Pride.

McHale was almost unstoppable. He was 6'11", and his extra-long arms and a variety of spins, ducks, leaps and soft shots made it impossible for any forward in the league to handle him from his favorite spot on the right side of the basket.

For several seasons the Celtics rotated Bird, McHale and Cedric Maxwell through the front line, and they simply wore out defenses. Parish had elevated his offensive game after so-so seasons with Golden State, and his superlative rebounding helped to trigger the Celtics' attack.

Auerbach made two more shrewd moves. He drafted guard Danny Ainge knowing that he wanted to play baseball, and waited until he gave up a budding major league career. He traded for guard Dennis Johnson in 1984 to shore up what was then a glaring need: a big guard to handle Andrew Toney of the 76ers, the Celtics' chief conference rival. D. J. immediately helped spark Boston to an NBA championship.

After losing to the Lakers in six games in 1985, the Celtics got their third – and last – title victory the following year, beating Houston in the championship series.

The retired jersey numbers of that decade's stars will hang right next to those of its other dynasty in the rafters of the new Boston Garden where the old parquet floor will still have its sundry soft spots and that mischievous leprechaun will live beneath the Celtics logo.

THE CHICAGO BULLS, 1991-93

Michael Jordan was probably the most important single player to his team's fortunes since Bill Russell contributed to the Boston Celtics' great dynasty because, like Russell, he could control a game by himself.

But the Bulls' dominance in the early nineties wasn't attributable only to Jordan.

The Bulls had great direction from coach Phil Jackson, who seemed impervious to the raging flow of egos around him; and whose most brilliant move may have been hiring veteran coaches Johnny Bach and Tex Winter to handle the strategy.

Jordan had excellent support also, from Scottie Pippen and Horace Grant, and a well-balanced cast of reserves

and role players – the Jordanaires – as they began moving toward their dominance by making the Eastern Conference finals in 1989 and 1990, and then winning three straight NBA titles.

Unlike Russell, whose major contributions to the Celtics' dynasty were on defense, Jordan excelled at both ends of the court. His 30-point average led all Chicago scorers and he also made the NBA's all-defensive team.

But Jordan had already proved he couldn't do it by himself, and it wasn't until both Pippen and Grant matured as players in the 1991 season – and after Cartwright arrived to play center in 1989 – that Chicago became a champion.

Everyone else fit in. John Paxson joined Jordan in the

Left: It wasn't until players such as Scottie Pippen arrived to help Michael Jordan that the Chicago Bulls put together three consecutive NBA titles, from 1991 to 1993.

Opposite top: Horace Grant (54) added the rebounding strength and inside scoring that Chicago needed to give Jordan more leeway for his offense.

Opposite: Jordan (23) was the most spectacular player of his era with his array of swooping, soaring, driving shots, and his tenacious defense.

Opposite far right: Jordan battled Charles Barkley and the Phoenix Suns in the 1993 NBA Finals to produce the Bulls' third straight title.

backcourt, bringing his cool resolve and good outside shooting. Will Perdue was an adequate backup center, and young players like B. J. Armstrong, Stacy King and Scott Williams added depth.

Jordan, Pippen and Grant were the only players who averaged double figures in scoring during those three championship seasons - even non-playoff teams had more big scorers – but such was Jordan's dominance that everyone else's contributions fit nicely into the entire picture.

The Bulls won two of their titles in relative ease. They gleefully dispatched Detroit in five games in the 1991 conference championship, then defeated the Lakers in five games for their first NBA title. The picture is forever vivid in the memories of basketball fans of Jordan cradling the NBA championship trophy as if it was a newborn babe.

Chicago then knocked off the Portland Trail Blazers in six games the following year, breaking a 2-2 tie with two straight wins.

"The first one was for the city itself," Jordan said. "We won it for the people of Chicago. The second one was for the players and coaches."

The third one might have been for himself because he put on one of the greatest single NBA Finals performances ever seen as Chicago beat the Phoenix Suns in six games. It was the first time a team had won three consecutive NBA championships since the 1960s. Two months later Jordan retired and the Bulls were left to compete on their own in 1994 – and didn't do badly with the NBA's fourth best record.

Left: After Jordan led the Bulls to their third straight title in 1993, he bade farewell to the game – but with the admission that he might return.

Below: A dynasty on display: From left, Michael Jordan, Bill Cartwright and Scottie Pippen display the Bulls' three NBA Championship trophies.

INDEX